1

# Smith's Heart Of Man
## *Repair Manual*

# Bill Smith

ISBN:
eBook: 978-1-7369800-0-2
Paperback: 978-1-7369800-1-9
AudioBook: 978-1-7369800-2-6

First paperback edition June 2021

Book design by *William G. Smith III*

Published by William G. Smith III / Flawed Ink Publishing
FlawedInk.com

# Table Of Contents

# Chapter 0
## Greetings And Salutations

I'm not quite sure why on that dreary, mundane Monday afternoon this subject was brought to my attention. I was walking down the unfamiliar aisle of the housewares section of a popular department store accompanying my lifelong friend, Jeremy, who was in search of a coffee pot. This machine was necessary to supply the much-needed caffeinated beverage coursing through his veins at the proper ratio. Our search was yielding no results and I was becoming increasingly frustrated; as it was at that moment that this simple yet profound question hit me like a ton of bricks:

**"What the hell happened to the men in our society?"**

I thought, *What an odd question*, when it initially came to me. Different theories and plausible explanations drifted through my mind at that moment, and I made a few feeble attempts at solving this riddle. However, I came to believe my observation was intended to probe a little deeper in to the psyche of our contemporary societal morays.

It doesn't take a genius to realize that the traditional image of what a man is considered to be has been put into question and severely diminished in recent years. One could even make a reasonably convincing argument that the role of what a man is, or should be, has been cleverly and deliberately eroded long before that.

You see, I find myself at somewhat of a crossroads in my life. I was born in the late 1970's; the ass end of Generation X and the embryonic stages of Generation Y. I've heard and studied the mighty exploits of "The Greatest Generation," of which my grandparents belonged. The generation of men who conquered the evil Axis of power and saved our planet from tyrannical evil. They had a hand in introducing liberty throughout the world along with introducing innovations in technology—the likes of which had never been seen before. They created a freer and more prosperous society for all. Or so the history books tell us.

However, I was raised by Baby Boomers. A generation in which half of its men fought, and died in a country a world away, in a war that was waged for incomprehensible reasons. A vast majority of those men who did not fight tuned in, turned on, and then dropped out. They denounced and spit on their fellow countrymen upon their arrival home.

As of late, I find myself being surrounded by Millennials. A promising, but wayward generation that appears to have all the advantages, and privileges the former generations endeavored so hard to obtain for them, yet none of the common sense, or intestinal fortitude to responsibly and properly wield said advantages, and privileges.

Recently I experienced what some often allude to as a "moment of clarity," where I had the following epiphany: I've evolved into the person Bob Seger sang about in his seminal anthem *Old Time Rock and Roll*. The singer can no longer relate to current trends and yearns for the simpler pleasure of yesteryear. That being said, it is quite possible that I am beginning to enter the throes of a full-blown middle-aged crisis. Hell! Even I admit the thought crossed my mind a time or two.

However, upon further personal reflection, I came to this conclusion: It isn't a middle-aged crisis I was encountering, rather an understanding that men, and proper patriarchal roles in society have been on a serious downturn.

And like so many of you gentlemen, I had become a reluctant, and unknowing victim to this crime.

There are many things that can be attributed to this phenomenon.

The decline of the family in western civilization. The creation of modern, and computerized industries. It could also be attributed to a drifting away from practicing of traditional spiritual and moral observances.

The intention of this is not to pin point and assess blame of how we misplaced or surrendered our identities and purposes as men. Rather, it is to go on an individual, and then collective quest to rediscover and reclaim our lost or suppressed masculine statuses and roles.

We need to look long and hard into a mirror and ask ourselves the difficult questions that we have either been avoiding, or didn't even think we needed to answer. It's time we suck it up. Let's put on our big boy pants, stop being butt hurt about everything, and contend for the very life and breath of why we were created. Morpheus is handing us the red pill.

## Men Are Important, Yet Unaware.

That fact is extremely significant, but remains hidden from most of us. I want to share a brief exert from a commentary given by talk show host, Tucker Carlson, which puts some skin to the bones of what we are discussing:

"The average American man will die five years before the average American woman. One of the reasons for this is addiction. Men are more than twice as likely as women to become alcoholics. They're also twice as likely to die of a drug OD. In New Hampshire, one of the states hit hardest by the opioid crisis, 73 percent of overdose deaths were men. But the saddest reason for shortened life spans is suicide. Seventy-seven percent of all suicides are committed by men. The overall rate is increasing at a dramatic pace. Between 1997 and 2014, there was a 43 percent rise in suicide deaths among middle-aged American men. The rates are highest among American Indian and white men, who kill themselves at about ten times the rate of Hispanic and black women. You often hear of America's incarceration crisis. That's almost exclusively a male problem too. Over 90 percent of inmates are male.

These problems are complex, and they start young. Relative to girls, boys are failing in school. More girls than boys graduate high school. Considerably more go to and graduate from college. Boys account for the overwhelming majority of school discipline cases. One study found that fully one in five high school boys had been diagnosed with hyperactivity disorder, compared with just one in 11 girls. Many were medicated for it. The long-term health effects of those medications aren't fully understood, but they appear to include depression in later life. Women decisively outnumber men in graduate school. They earn the majority of doctoral degrees.

They are now the majority of new enrollees in both law and medical schools.

For men, the consequences of failing in school are profound.

Between 1979-2010, working-age men with only high school degrees saw their real hourly wages drop about 20 percent. Over the same period, high school educated women saw their wages rise. The decline of the industrial economy disproportionately hurt men. There are now 7 million working-age American men who are no longer in the labor force. They've dropped out. Nearly half of them take pain medication on any given day. That's the highest rate in the world by far.

Far fewer young men get married than did just a few decades ago, and fewer stay married. About one in five American children live with only their mothers. That's double the rate in 1970. Millions more boys are growing up without fathers. Young adult men are now more likely to live with a parent than with a spouse or partner. That is not the case for young women. Single women buy their own homes at more than twice the rate of single men. More women than men now have drivers licenses."

As if that was not disconcerting enough, Carlson continues:

"Even physically men are falling behind. A recent study found that almost half of young men failed the Army's entry-level physical fitness test during basic training. Fully seventy percent of American men are overweight or obese, as compared to 59 percent of American women.

Perhaps most terrifyingly, men seem to be becoming less male — fundamentally, measurably. Sperm counts across the west have plummeted, down almost 60 percent since the early 1970s. Scientists don't know why. Testosterone levels in men have also fallen precipitously. One study found that the average levels of male testosterone dropped by 1 percent every year after 1987. And it is unrelated to age. The average 40-year-old-man in 2017 would have testosterone levels 30 percent lower than the average 40-year-old man in 1987.

There is no upside to this trend. Lower testosterone levels in men are associated with depression, lethargy, weight gain and decreased cognitive ability. Nothing like this has ever happened to a population this big. You'd think we'd want to know what exactly is going on and how to fix it. Yet the media ignores the story. It's considered a fringe topic."[1]

**Gentlemen, This Is Not Good.**

We've been virtue signaled into believing that our worth is admitting you're bad and our default position is like a dog panting at his master's feet. We need to get some testicular fortitude and foster an environment where this sentiment will flourish and thrive amongst all men. We can no longer acquiesce to the feeble-minded in our society that are threatened by the slightest traces of men utilizing their God-given abilities. No more apologizing for who or what we are. We do not need sensitivity training; we need to learn how to be a man.

Cowering and giving into these demands will only embolden these feebleminded, confused souls. No more pandering to those whiny cry baby's that operate under the auspicious of "the squeaky wheel gets the oil," in the attempt to shut us up. It is time we help and lead them. When it comes to the scourge of this politically correct, social justice nonsense that seeks to knee cap and castrate us as a gender, surrender is not an option. Our choices: scurry away in utter embarrassment or simply man up.

As a man, you set the tone for the relationships you have in your life. Men by design are leaders. We are supposed to guide ourselves, and those around us in a noble and righteous direction. We must learn how to taper male aggression and lethargy and channel them into assertiveness.

This is not intended to be—nor should it ever come across—as chauvinistic or sexist. It is not our demeaning attitudes but our qualities that make us men. Not every leader is a man. However, every man is a leader. We need to ask ourselves if we are leading effectively or not. When men begin to stand up and contend to rightly fulfill our roles, everyone throughout our sphere of influence begins to ascend alongside of us. Remember this:

## Toxic Masculinity Is Not Real Masculinity

The two dominant masculine role models in my life were Jesus, and my father. Their teachings and examples, have helped shaped a fairly well rounded man. I realize that many guys weren't as fortunate as I to have such strong male role models helping to navigate the choppy waters of life. My moral compass was pointed to true north at a very early age and their guidance, love, and correction hasn't failed me.

Gentlemen, I thank you for taking the time to read this book. Together we will be embarking on this quest to rediscover nan's missing attributes. If this can in any way help you come closer to the man you want to be, and helps you fulfill the goals in your life, then I will be far more grateful than I am able to express within my limited vocabulary.

# Chapter 1
## Definition and Quality

**definition** / *noun* / "the act of defining, or of making something definite, distinct, or clear"[1]

As I explained in chapter 0, we are going on this quest to understand and reclaim what the authentic essence of being a man is all about. This quest will start now and finish once you take your final breath. Truth is, as far as I can attest, you will continue to grow, learn, be challenged, and confounded for the rest of your life. And as we observe in nature, whatever isn't growing is dying. These obstacles placed in our paths are precisely what God and life use in the grand experiment called the human condition. As you have already noticed, there are no safe zones in life. Life is a battle from which there is no retreat or surrender.

I am a firm believer in transparency, setting realistic expectations, and understanding objectives — especially pertaining to the specific goal or mission at hand. This means getting to the core of what the definition of a man is and what authentic manliness is about. There is a vast difference between being born a male and developing and growing into a man. Let us examine the definitions of some important words so we can revisit them as we continue on this quest.

**male** / *noun* / "a person bearing an X and Y chromosome pair in the cell nuclei and normally having a penis, scrotum, and testicles, and developing hair on the face at adolescence; a boy or man."[2]

Biologically, a male is a person born with different chromosomes and unique physical attributes that differentiates himself from females. When it comes down to the actual molecular and fleshly components that are pieced together to create a individual being, there are many physical distinctions, characteristics and attributes that separate a male from a female. If we are separated in this capacity, then logic should dictate that there are different, if not opposite, purposes and functions between a male and female. These differences are found within our genetic compositions as well as our spiritual and mental capabilities. Or in other words, to quote the film *Kindergarten Cop*, "Boys have a penis, and girls have a vagina."[3]

Modern cultural pundits would have you believe that statements such as these run into a "gray area." For example, it might be viewed as being insensitive to gender fluidity. They could also be perceived as antiquated roles that each sex plays. I would argue that the farther away we get from our true biological identities, the deeper we delve into confusion. Lost in contemporary societal mosaics that allow for contradictions in items, which are diametrically opposed to one another, to co-exist in some form of false reality. Author George Orwell referred to it as "doublethink."

In contradiction to the word "male," we find the definition of the word "man."

**Man** / *noun* / "a man or boy who shows the qualities (such as strength and courage) that men are traditionally supposed to have"[4]

## Quality Merchandise

The primary difference in definition between "male" and "man" are external versus internal. We see the meaning of "male" is essentially having the ability to grow a beard and having a Johnson. While a "man" has qualities like strength and courage.

To break this down, we need to focus on this specific word: qualities. To me the word *qualities*, or just *quality*, is very interesting. Ultimately, it deals with worth or value. Here is the definition:

**quality** / *noun* / 1. an essential or distinctive characteristic, property, or attribute:
2. character or nature, as belonging to or distinguishing a thing:
3. character with respect to fineness, or grade of excellence:

4. high grade; superiority; excellence:
5. a personality or character trait [5]

The first time I attempted to purchase a piece of jewelry I knew absolutely nothing. Especially when it came to understanding true quality. There is a lot that goes into it, and I was overwhelmed at my utter ignorance on the subject. With gold, the primary issue is the purity, or quality, of it. Will it be 14, 18, or 24 karats? The higher the karat number, the purer the gold is, which dictates the price. These combined qualities, when calculated together are what composes the final cost and value. The higher the quality, the higher the price. Just like anything in life, quality will cost you.

There are processes that need to happen in order to find these beautiful diamonds and pure gold. Which are often grueling and uncomfortable. Hard work, and research goes into procuring these natural elements and transforming them into usable objects. Only after all of that can people craft them into the beautiful things we adorn our loved ones with as a gesture of our unfailing faith and devotion.

The Bible compares the process of refining gold, to the process we as men go through life developing our quality:

"Rejoice in this, even though for a little while you may have to experience grief in various trials. Even gold is tested for genuineness by fire. The purpose of these trials is so that your trust's genuineness, which is far more valuable than perishable gold, will be judged worthy of praise, glory and honor at the revealing of Yeshua the Messiah."

1 Peter 1:6-7[6] CJB

When I was in high school, I was enrolled in industrial technologies. Four years of mechanical drawing, wood, and metal shop. I *loved* metal shop. The smell of steel, the visceral sensation of beating the hell out of various blocks of metal into usable shapes, the dust particles flying throughout the air that most certainly were not recommended for anyone to inhale (*let alone young, still maturing, teenagers*). David Pardington was my teacher for all four years and he became one of many foundational men in my life. I learned plenty from him, not only about metallurgy but music, the Blues, and carrying oneself like a man. I learned how to operate lathes, welding equipment, and other machinery. Looking back at it now, it is nothing but Providence that I am alive and still have the usage of many parts of my body.

One of the mechanisms we learned to operate was a foundry. It was much smaller than the industrial ones used to refine metals for commercial purposes, but the principle was still the same. The entire process typically went like this: You melt different metals until they become liquefied, then pour that into casts. After the metal cooled, you remove the item it from the cast, and there you have it.

The process was tedious and lengthy. Normally it took one class to create the mold, and then another class to melt and pour the liquid metal into the mold. Much care, preparation, and safety went into melting the metal and then pouring it into the mold.

Then we had to suit up. There were these specially-insulated, heat-resistant vests, pant and shoe coverings, bulky gloves, and tinted heat shields (*to protect our face from melting off*). Not only were they cumbersome to put on, but you could barely do anything while wearing them. And just to add a tad more discomfort and embarrassment, they were the brightest yellow known to man. I'm talking highlighter yellow on steroids, multiplied by a thousand (*I think the reason our eye shields were tinted was to prevent blindness caused by looking at the freaking things*).

This was a required project, so everybody had to endure the hellacious process at least twice a year, once for yourself, and then once to help a classmate. An interesting thing occurs after you have selected and created your mold. You had to choose the kind of metal you were going to use which could change the outcome of your project drastically. This is because different metals melt at different temperatures, thus the primary reason we often used aluminum. It melted at a relatively low temperature, and was a lot quicker than steel or iron to liquify. Throughout the entire process you notice that the imperfections from the metal begins to float and collect at the top. Once enough has collected, you simply scrape it off and continue. The higher quality metals don't have as many impurities in them as the cheaper ones, but all had some. It is the heat that causes the metal to release its imperfections and rise to the top of the cauldron to be properly removed. If those impurities are not discarded before you pour your mold, it will make your object malformed and useless.

What I learned in metal shop is applicable to all humans, but this example should be especially relatable to men. We have to be tried by the fires of life to have the junk in our heart removed so we can be made pure. This is what the scripture above alluded to. Many times in life we encounter people, and circumstances that are difficult. We may wish these things away, but rarely do they ever depart us so easily.

Once we realize that these struggles are the very occurrences that lead to our purification, causing us to become a higher-quality individual, the quicker we can move past them. This has been my experience, as well as many of the men in my life that I value and look up to. The fact of the matter is in life, much like in metallurgy, you have to endure heat and pressure if you want to be rid of the things that deteriorate and devalue us.

## Faramir's Quality

A fantastic example of quality is the story of Faramir in *The Lord Of the Rings* film trilogy, based on the books by J.R.R. Tolkien and directed by Peter Jackson. Tolkien dives into great detail concerning every angle and plot point throughout his influential literary masterpiece. Tolkien's story of the evil Ring of power and the Fellowship who seek to destroy and end its villainous reign, is full of heroism, allusions to spirituality, and moral truths that transcend time, culture, and technology.

Faramir's experience with the Ring began when he met Frodo and his companion Sam. Faramir being Captain of the Guard captured them just as they would any trespasser. Upon discovering that Frodo and Sam had The Ring in their possession, Faramir's heart began to be tempted by the same evil that had intoxicated so many others. He knew full well that such a magnificent gift if presented to the Steward, who coincidentally was his father, would surely gain favor in his eyes.

By this time, the weight of the Ring was taking an exhaustive toll on Frodo. As Faramir attempted to take the Ring, Frodo lashed out at him, surprising everyone in the camp. Sam reasoned with Faramir, he shared with him the story of a man named Boromir whose heart had been betrayed by The Ring, which ultimately lead to his demise, who unbeknownst to both of them was Faramir's brother. Sam pleaded with Faramir to release them so they could continue upon their quest. If the Steward found out Faramir had let such a valuable item go, he would be disavowed. With the severity of this decision at hand, Faramir made the difficult choice to not just release them, but to aid them on their journey. As they parted ways Sam said, "Captain Faramir, you have shown your quality, sir - the very highest."[7]

You see, it isn't always the mighty and brave demonstrations that define what a man's quality consists of. Being a man of great quality has less to do with the outward appearance and actions, and more to do with the inward condition of our heart and attitude. Making a decision that reflects your quality is the ability to see past oneself and the longings of his heart.

The two other words in the definition of a man, along with quality, were strength and courage. You can take these definitions at face value, but the further along we go on our quest, you will realize that one cannot simply paint these terms with broad strokes. Strength and courage come in many shapes, and sizes. Manhood, we discover, is much like the rest of life: it's all about balance.

## The Man In The Arena

As I close this chapter, I want you to ask yourself two things:

**1.** What qualities define true manliness and what is my perception of those qualities?
**2.** What qualities have I overlooked, dismissed, or neglected on my quest?

Being a man isn't easy, that's why many males refuse to evolve into one. Many homo-sapiens that were born with the physical attributes of a male may have developed physically, but have not invested the time to cultivate the qualities necessary to become a man.

Let me leave you with this quote from President Theodore "Teddy" Roosevelt. I find there is something intrinsic to being a man that lies within this brief passage. For it is not in victory or defeat, luxury or poverty, health or illness, that a man's quality is defined. It is defined in his heart and acknowledged in is deeds. It is cultivated through the processes it took for him to achieve the inevitable outcome that propels him forward. Through the victory, as well as the defeat. Through the extravagant, as well as the humblest of season in his life. Through physical fitness and physical lack. The attempted and continual effort, regardless of rewards or accolades, that demands he be devoted wholly to what is right, is the very essence of a man. Whether he succeeds or fails is of no consequence, it is the fact that he tries and refuses to surrender. Men allow your quality to shine through and be looked upon continually as an example to all.

"It is not the critic who counts; not the man who points out how the strong man stumbles, or where the doer of deeds could have done them better. The credit belongs to the man who is actually in the arena, whose face is marred by dust and sweat and blood; who strives valiantly; who errs, who comes short again and again, because there is no effort without error and shortcoming; but who does actually strive to do the deeds; who knows great enthusiasms, the great devotions; who spends himself in a worthy cause; who at the best knows in the end the triumph of high achievement, and who at the worst, if he fails, at least fails while daring greatly, so that his place shall never be with those cold and timid souls who neither know victory nor defeat."[8]

# Chapter 2
## Character

character / *noun* / 1. "the aggregate of features and traits that form the individual nature of some person or thing.
2. moral or ethical quality

character / *adjective* / 3. qualities of honesty, courage, or the like; integrity
4. a person represented in a drama, story, etc."[1]

Ah, character. Such an odd little word. It's definition, like many of us, carries a duality by its very nature. We contend with the notion of what exactly character is, not only generationally, but culturally as well. There is an underlying internal struggle that I would argue most, if not all, wrestle with. As we turn to the exact meaning of the word, we find that it is descriptive in two primary, yet distinct areas. The first, dealing with the individual condition of one's heart. The second, dealing with the portrayal of a character cast in a role, or if I may, the public persona of one's self. There is a vast difference between *having* character, and *being a* character.

Character, much like quality, is one of those things that can be difficult to define, but very obvious to recognize. I have long believed that the choices a man makes, is the greatest reflection of his character. Whether your character is noble or deplorable, there will be no need to broadcast it. Time will make it obvious to all. Be it good or bad. People acknowledge when they find something that is good, especially when they have been purposely seeking for it.

So often we are attracted to a personality type or trait, but it doesn't always match or properly convey the character of the person. Case and point: We all know someone who is the life of a party. This person is a hoot to be around, and everyone usually has a ball when they grace any given situation with their presence. Be that as it may, you know they are not someone who you would intentionally choose to spend your free time with. It could be from many different things you have deduced about them. Such as, you wouldn't trust them as far as you could throw them, or perhaps they are the kind of person that would sell their mother out for a buck. You just know either from personal experience, or secondhand news, that their character is less than desirable.

There is a great divide between having character and being one. In my opinion, most people play a character, because frankly, it is just easier. Authenticity of character is a very rare and precious thing. It takes years of living, and perseverance to develop. None of us are born with character that reflects consistent quality; it is something that has to be nurtured and cultivated as we continue through this quest of life.

How do you differentiate someone with quality of character, versus someone playing a character? That's the tricky part. Dr. Hannibal Lecter is a character created by Thomas Harris and appeared in a series of novels he wrote. Dr. Lecter was most notably portrayed by Sir Anthony Hopkins in several films including *The Silence of the Lambs*. I have never met Mr. Hopkins, but I assume that he is neither a forensic psychiatrist nor a cannibalistic serial killer.

You could be saying to yourself, "Bill this is a very extreme example. I mean how many people are actually going to befriend and engage in relationship with that kind of person? Well let me ask you a few questions. Have you ever met anyone who studied people to use them to gain access to what they wanted in order to fulfill their selfish ambitions? Have you ever known someone that you trusted, then later on destroyed that trust once their true character and motives were revealed? If you look at it through this lens, it isn't too hard to see the correlation.

I can think of a few people I have encountered through the course of my life that were very much like that. Many friends and acquaintances have had their mental, emotional, and spiritual lives destroyed by such behavior demonstrated on behalf of others who have operated in this vein.

The truth is, that there are many ways to inflict pain on someone. Quite often, inflicting a physical injury, in the long run, is the least painful option, with the fewest side effects. It is the emotional toll, and spiritual abuses that often foster the most persistent and damaging. In the past I have allowed people access in my life that hurt me. There is no shame in that. If you're being honest for a moment, I am sure you can relate. The question isn't *if it happened*, rather *what did you do after it happened?*

We need to be wise about who we allow into our circle of trust. The scriptures warn us:

> "Do not be so deceived *and* misled! Evil companionships (communion, associations) corrupt *and* deprave good manners *and* morals *and* character."
>
> 1 Corinthians 15:33[2] AMP

Birds of a feather flock together. You are known by the company you keep. It is all essentially saying the same thing: The people we let into our lives have the ability to influence the kind of person we are or will become.

**The Elusive Character Club**

Author H. Jackson Brown, Jr. said that, "Our character is what we do when we think no one is looking."[3] We know this is a process, and the most difficult part of the process is getting started. The Bible teaches us about the development of good character:

"Not only so, but we also glory in our sufferings, because we know that suffering produces perseverance; perseverance, character; and character, hope."

Romans 5:3-4[4] NIV

Suffering, or enduring the hardships of life, allows us to carry on. As we persevere through adversity, it begins the process of character development. Character, gives us the audacity to realize that we CAN make it through catastrophes, with strength of character, which ends up resulting in hope. It is hope that propels us forward in life. It also grants us access to *The Elusive Character Club.*

It's elusive because many people in our society do not know how to gain (*or that they should even aspire for*) upright character that influences and inspires people. So many men have just checked out. They are arrested in a perpetual state of undeveloped character. This applies to young men as well as old. Truthfully, what I have observed is the more seasoned of us gents are normally the ones that have stalled out in this process. We've gotten stuck in a rut and had neither the will nor desire to be freed.

Taking the easy way out, letting someone else fight our own battles, being wooed by lesser lovers, and settling for ordinary, while extraordinary is within our grasp... These are the character killers in our lives.

Businessman Les Brown said, "Our ability to handle life's challenges is a measure of our strength of character."[5]

Claiming we have good character without having good character is like pissing in the wind: messy and stupid. Here is a verse that's worthy of our aim:

"But the fruit of the Spirit [the result of His presence within us] is love [unselfish concern for others], joy, [inner] peace, patience [not the ability to wait, but how we act while waiting], kindness, goodness, faithfulness, gentleness, self-control. Against such things there is no law."

Galatians 5:22-23[6] AMP

This is commonly referred to as the "Fruits of the Spirit." They are a detailed list of attributes that will help us develop good character. So let's unpack this. We got love, or unselfish concern for others. That's a fantastic thing, no? Joy and inner peace, good stuff there. I bet you can use a bit more of that? How we act while we wait is the best definition of patience in character development I've ever heard. We also have kindness, goodness, faithfulness, gentleness, and self-control. Now if we are honest, we all need these qualities in our lives.

When I was just a wee young lad, I played every sport that I could. Baseball, basketball, football, wrestling, and track and field (*though I mostly stayed off the track and stuck to the field*).

Playing sports was primarily a great way for my dad and I to bond. Thankfully, he was a coach for every team I played on, up until high school. I learned how to compete, be a good sport, the agony of defeat *(honestly, my teams rarely won)*, and I also got some exercise. A three hundred and sixty degree win. I do look back on those times with great fondness and warmth.

I played football up until tenth grade. Junior Varsity, was pretty much fun and games. It was cool to hang with my friends, be a part of the pep rallies, get invited to parties, and be showered with all the accolades that accompany it. Those spoils were even applicable to a chubby bench warmer like yours truly. (*I mean chicks dig the uniform. Am I right, or am I right?*). In tenth grade however, everything changed. Varsity high school football was an entirely different beast altogether.

Playtime was over—no more fun and games. We had new coaches, a different field, and a new locker room. The practice schedule increased as well. I was accustomed to the lighthearted two-hour evening practice routine. No more of that for this little cupcake. Practices were jacked up to the infamous two-a-day schedule, which were exponentially more grueling. This was not good news for my underachieving ears to hear, and it was unbearable for my plump tookus to endure.

I hated the intense competition, and the fact that my lifelong friends and I weren't solely the kings of the field any longer. We were forced to compete for not only our positions, but even our numbers. OUR NUMBERS FOR THE LOVE OF GOD! The upperclassmen were ruthless because they were older, and basically could get away with it. I mean who was going to stop them? The coaches? Hell no! They encouraged that behavior. We got hazed. I know that kind of thing isn't suppose to happen anymore, but let me tell you, if I had a dollar for every time I got a wedgie, rug-burn, or titty twister, I would be a very rich man. I played nose guard on defense and center on offense. And of course, as luck would have it, or maybe you could chalk it up to Murphy's Law, an upperclassmen had not only both positions but my number too (*Things like that just happen to me*).

During tryouts I had to compete against *Vince*. It was awful, he was awful, and he treated me equally as awful. Vince was a behemoth of a kid, and that's saying something coming from me. He was cocky and had proven himself on the football field, and also had a rather attractive girlfriend (*See? I told you chicks dig the uniform*). Imagine if you will, a towering, pimply-faced behemoth that had horrendous body odor, bad breath, and farts that rivaled that of the most insidiously putrid landfill. Put that all together and there was *Vince*. He took great delight in handing out punishments of a wide variety. I truly believed that his sole purpose for living was to beat the living crap out of me whenever the opportunity arose. I had my ass handed to me during tryouts, over and over again. I lost the number I had for three years. Don't even bother wondering if I had a chance at either position. I did, however, earn third string bench warmer. In other words, the only time I was able to play during a game would be if we were up by a thousand points. I had ridden the pinewood express before, but I got to play enough that I was able to hold my head up high amongst my peers.

Needless to say, I loathed football, and I desperately wanted to quit. I begged my dad to let me leave the team. My mom, bless her heart, was persuaded rather easily when she saw the enormous bruises I had accumulated, courtesy of my varsity teammates. I thought surely, with my mom testifying for me and the copious amounts of physical scarring I admitted as evidence, I had presented nothing short of a rock solid case for which my dad would have no other course of action except to allow me to quit before season's end.

Instead, he stood and looked me square in the eyes and said "no," in a calm voice that was as irritating, as it was powerful. With pathetic, tear-filled eyes I pleaded, "Why?" He stood stoic and said very matter of factly, "You made a commitment to your coaches, your friends, your team, and your school to be there. And you will be there. If you want to quit after the season is over and never play again, go right ahead."
Groveling, I attempted to rebuttal with him, "But dad, no one cares. All I'm going to do is sit on the sidelines all season."

"I care, and so should you," he replied.

"But why, dad, I don't get it?"

My dad answered, "Because, son, that is what a man does. He sees his commitments through to the end and carries out his duties as best he can." And with those words, he drew that conversation to an end.

Those words impacted and shaped my life in such a profound way.

As I am sure you have already guessed, I finished out that season and thus my rather un-illustrious high school football days came to a close. Actually, it ended my high school sports career entirely. Although I got beat up everyday at practice and I didn't play one second all year, I began to notice something. One by one, many of my friends stopped coming to practice, and then to games. Then I saw something that was even more astonishing to me. As the years went on their behavior and status began to change. Most of it was just a bunch of high school kid chicanery, stupid stuff the majority of us do, but you could begin to see behavioral patterns develop. Not all, but many of them would buckle under peer pressure, and get into all sorts of trouble. Some got into drugs, thievery, impregnating their girlfriend or girlfriends, and a few even wound up in jail.

What my dad did was instill in me something that helped me become a man and cultivate good character throughout my life. He taught me accountability and that all you have in this life as a man is your word. Like Al Pacino said in *Scarface*, "All I have in this world is my balls and my word, and I don't break them for no one."[7]

Author Zig Ziglar puts it, "It was character that got us out of bed, commitment that moved us into action, and discipline that enabled us to follow through."[8]

As I reflect upon this, it was actually good for me that *Vince,* as well as the rest of the upperclassmen, treated me so harshly. Hindsight being 20/20 and all, I needed it. I was a spoiled infant who had always gotten his way. My overreaction was my attempt as a puberty-stricken brat to throw a temper-tantrum because I was being challenged with something that I had no control over. I wanted out because I did not have foresight to understand how that decision would impact my life. In fact, every time I took the easy route, or the road more commonly traveled as it were, I found I learned little if nothing at all that was any benefit to me long term. I have always said that I have learned far more from my mistakes than I ever have from any successes.

I could give you a couple dozen stories, and cliché sayings, but I already know that you are as smart as I am, and most likely smarter, and handsomer (*Look at you, you handsome devil*). I also know beyond the shadow of a doubt that The Almighty endowed you with the capacity to figure these things out, all by your little old lonesome. Humans as a species have an innate ability to comprehend, and be stretched farther, then all of God's other creations.

Picture in your mind for a moment a man that you know who is worthy of your admiration. A stalwart fella you trust, value, and cherish, all that he has done and spoken into your life. Someone you strive to emulate. I hope somewhere along the span of your life you have encountered just such a man. If you haven't, consider some men in history, or popular culture that have these attributes.

If we really stop and think about it, we should innately know what the difference between right or wrong is. How a man ought to behave, and what is expected of a man who is virtuous and commendable. This doesn't necessarily mean we always hit the mark or get a home run every time we're at bat. It just means that you give a damn about yourself and others, and that you strive to accomplish and live up to your potential and abilities, one hundred percent of the time. Like Heavy Weight Champ Evander Holyfield said, "It is not the size of a man but the size of his heart that matters."[9]

## Character Speaks Louder Than Words

You could simply assume someone with bad character is a jerk, but I think that is really just an oversimplification of a much deeper issue. Why is this person a jerk? What series of events have prompted or encouraged them to continue on in their state of jerkiness? It isn't enough to just say to someone "stop being a jerk." Admitting there is a problem is the first, and most crucial step to take, in order to begin to rectify a deficiency of character, but it is not the only step to take. The following scripture highlights traits and behaviors that you should try to avoid:

"Don't be naive. There are difficult times ahead. As the end approaches, people are going to be self-absorbed, money-hungry, self-promoting, stuck-up, profane, contemptuous of parents, crude, coarse, dog-eat-dog, unbending, slanderers, impulsively wild, savage, cynical, treacherous, ruthless, bloated windbags, addicted to lust, and allergic to God. They'll make a show of religion, but behind the scenes they're animals. Stay clear of these people."

2 Timothy 3:1-5[10] MSG

Good character takes into consideration how a man's words and deeds will shape and guide those who have allowed him into their sphere of influence. It's not just enough to do and say the right thing when it is expected. Those are just exercises in futility (*kind of like playing leap frog with an unicorn*). It is unsustainable, and dangerous. A man's true character is something that he takes and models with him everywhere he goes.

This doesn't mean we will score 100% on all of life's tests. We will behave poorly and act like over-bloated windbags from time to time. Cultivation of good character is a deliberate and steady exploration into the root of the problem in our hearts. As we begin to acknowledge where these negative traits started, we will be able to eliminate them. That is how we win and cultivate good character in our lives: step-by-step. We gain victory and take command over these impulses. Eventually, we may even remove them entirely.

Dr. Seuss famously said, "Unless someone like you cares a whole awful lot, nothing is going to get better. It's not."[11] What Dr. Seuss was saying is that you are the only one who can choose to change yourself. More importantly the impact of the character you exhibit will be the most fitting tribute of your time here on Earth. Take responsibility for yourself, and choices you have made, be it good or bad. Then learn from those decisions and move forward accordingly. This is what men do.

Remember this: it is a lot easier to burn a house down than to build one from the bottom up. Most will light the match instead of picking up the hammer. I offered you two lists of attributes, one that fosters good character and one that does not. But it is up to you to decide what kind of character you want to be remembered for. Theologian Charles Spurgeon offered this observation:

"A good character is the best tombstone. Those who loved you and were helped by you will remember you when forget-me-nots have withered. Carve your name on hearts, not on marble."[12]

# Chapter 3
## Integrity

integrity / *noun* / 1. adherence to moral and ethical principles;
soundness of moral character; honesty.
2. the state of being whole, entire, or undiminished[1]

While writing this chapter, I thought about how building a house is a great analogy for integrity. Quality and character are the firm foundation for us to build upon. Integrity is the framework we use to shape and give support throughout the structure.

As a man, your quality and character are demonstrated to the world when people see you. Integrity is what your heart consists of. The Bible says:

"He who walks in integrity *and* with moral character walks securely, But he who takes a crooked way will be discovered *and* punished."

Proverbs 10:9[2] AMP

Integrity has to do with the moral character of your heart. Do you know the old adage "honesty is the best policy." How about this one? "Tell the truth always, it's easier to remember than a lie." These proverbs are well-worn, and trustworthy just as we ought to be. If your character gets branded with a lack of integrity, it's hard to repair once damaged. Notice I said *hard*, not *impossible*. Be that as it may, a lack of integrity can become a stigma that sticks to you like glue. I'm sorry, gentlemen, but truth and fashion rarely intersect at a convenient junction.

## Relational Integrity

It is not surprising that integrity is so closely associated with structures. Have you ever heard something to the effect of "this buildings integrity has been damaged"? When you step into a building, you trust that it will not collapse once you've entered it. You trust that as you move from room to room and from floor to floor, the integrity of the structure will accompany you throughout. As people enter into relationship with us, they must be built upon integrity. What you need to ask yourself is, "Can people trust the relational integrity of what they have been constructing with me?"

But what exactly is relational integrity? How do you know if you have that with someone? If I damaged it, how can I repair it? These are valid and necessary questions you should be asking yourself.

Reggae Musician Bob Marley puts it like this, "The greatness of a man is not in how much wealth he acquires, but in his integrity and his ability to affect those around him positively."[3] Relational integrity means you can't bargain, or deceive someone, into having confidence in you. One's possessions and thinly-woven narratives are not what compel people to trust the integrity of relationships.

How do I know if I have relational integrity with someone else? The best way to answer that question is to evaluate your intentions of the relationship in an honest way. Am I being one-sided? Am I in this relationship for what I can get from it? Is the give and take equal? Is this mutually beneficial to both parties involved? Whatever questions you may ask yourself, hopefully you have come to the conclusion that it is all up to YOU, and the integrity that YOU bring to the relationship. I like how Novelist John D. MacDonald puts it, "Integrity is not a conditional word. It doesn't blow in the wind or change with the weather. It is your inner image of yourself, and if you look in there and see a man who won't cheat, then you know he never will."[4] Integrity is a choice you have to make, and a standard that you have to raise on your own. It mustn't be swayed by relational politics or circumstances. To answer the question, as long as you continue to welcome integrity into your relationships, it will remain. If the other individual at any point decides to lack integrity, that is not on you.

If you have damaged your integrity, how can you begin to repair it? When you have made mistakes, and you truly value someone and the relationship you have with them, own up to what you've done. Be a man. That's the point of this whole book and the quest we've embarked upon. Do what is required to make things right. Swallow your pride. Admit your wrongdoings or shortcomings. Then try the best you can to regain their trust. It may be a gut-wrenching process, but if making things right with this individual is important to you, you will do whatever it takes.

In part, integrity is owning up to mistakes and asking for forgiveness when you screw up. There is this false assumption that, as men, we shouldn't confess our mistakes. That admitting you made an error, wanting to make amends, and desiring absolution will somehow lessen you as a man. I call shenanigans on that. You never look small when you take the high road. We should take the following to heart:

"God opposes the proud but shows favor to the humble."

James 4:6b[5] NIV

Pride is in direct opposition of integrity. No one is asking for perfection, not even God. And just as you must ask for forgiveness, so must you forgive. By holding onto past hurts you are only damaging yourself. If someone messes you over, do your best to forgive them. But if this is an issue that keeps coming up with a certain individual, at some point you have to question that relationship. This is, as in all of these things, a two-way street.

## Protecting Integrity

I am an audiophile. Which is just a fancy name for someone who loves music and collects its various physical formats. In my neighborhood, there's a store that sells CD's, LP's, books, movies, and other miscellaneous items. I have become acquaintances with several of the employees there, but I am friends with only one: Matt.

Matt and I have known each other for a long time, and couldn't be more different. We are diametrically opposed in nearly every conceivable way. However, Matt's awesome, and I get super bummed whenever I go and he isn't working. I met Matt years ago at a retail chain coffee house/book/music store. Coffee is the cornerstone of our friendship, as is our mutual love for Pop culture, art, and sarcasm. We respect the others beliefs, and try not to push them on one another.

One weekend, there was a big sale going on in the entire store. I walked in, saw Matt and greeted him for a moment. Then as is my custom, I headed towards the music section. After I had my final selections in tow. I proceeded to the check out, and am welcomed by a pleasant new face. She rings up my purchases, and I am on my way.

As I step back, it hits me that the total was a lot lower then I was guessing it was going to be. I say "adios" to Matt and leave. I opened up my bag and pulled out the receipt before driving off. Come to find out, the pleasant new face, undercharged me by nearly $20.00. For the slightest of moments I thought, "YES! I pulled one over on *the man!*" Then I came back to my senses and realized that it was thievery if I didn't go back in and pay.

One could try to rationalize that it wasn't technically theft because I paid for part of my purchase, or that it was on the store, because the girl at the register messed up. That dog don't hunt. I went back in, found Matt, told him what happened, and his jaw dropped in amazement. He looked at the bag I handed him, and came to the same conclusion as I did. I told him I didn't want anyone to get into trouble, and that I just wanted to make it right, Matt was floored and gave me an additional ten percent off. All was right with the world.

I bring it up for this reason. Matt and I are friends. I am heterosexual and Christian. Matt is homosexual and doesn't prescribe to any specific spiritual philosophy. People tend to think that two such individuals wouldn't be able to engage in a friendship. Which is nonsense. We are the exact people that need to learn and grow from one another. Matt and I are also friends on Facebook, and about a week or so after the record store incident, he posted a article about a "pastor" of a Christian church who made some horrible and heartless comments.

The comments had to do with the terrorist attack that occurred at the Pulse Nightclub in Orlando, Florida, on June 12, 2016. In this particular attack, a radical Islamic terrorist targeted a LGBTQ nightclub killing forty-nine people and injured many more. Essentially this "pastor's" comment was that the people who were slain got what they deserved because of the life styles they were leading. It was the judgment of God garbage that is so frequently heard in these types of scenarios.

I could see Matt had a great sense of pain within the brief comment he shared. My heart was hurt by the loss of life, the hatred that was perpetrated against the victims, and with the "pastor's" message. I felt in my heart I should say something to Matt. I wasn't sure what to say, how to say it, or even if he would care to hear it. I sent him a private message and basically apologized for what this "pastor" said, and for Christendom's attitude in general. I assured Matt that God did not feel this way. That God is love and he sent his son Jesus into the world not to condemn it, but that through Him the world may be redeemed.

I waited not knowing if he would respond, and what he would say if he did. Matt finally got back to me and to my surprise was very kind and openhearted. He said that I was the only Christian he knew that was living out my faith authentically and that he appreciated my apology and friendship in his life. We continued our messaging for a few hours and eventually said we would see each other later.

The whole reason for telling this story was because Matt saw the integrity in my actions, and it was a reflection of my character. He was able to see that I am a person he can trust to stand with integrity. Even though he and I differ on so many subjects, integrity is one thing that transcends those differences. Had I not came back in to the store with those unpaid items, he may have never known about it. But if he did eventually somehow discovered what occurred, it would have destroyed my integrity in his eyes and lump me into the category as the "pastor" that was spreading the hateful messages. Since that day, our relationship has changed for the better.

Integrity is most often comprised of things that we do when no one is looking. This is precisely why we need to protect the integrity in our lives and do all we can to establish a standard. The thoughts and deeds in our hearts, the places where no one has an open window to survey, these are the places in which integrity can grow and be nourished or be choked out.

It's caring for others over yourself. It's remembering your wedding anniversary. It's demonstrating to your sons how to properly treat a woman. It's showing your daughters how a man should treat them and not to settle for less. It's keeping the promises you make. It's trying your damnedest to give your children the advantages in life you never had, and knowing that has less to do with your billfold and more to do with your heart. It's loving them enough to give them the discipline they need in order to become productive and moral citizens. It's adhering to the golden rule and treating others as you want to be treated. Basically this:

"If you know the right thing to do and don't do it, that, for you, *is* evil."

James 4:17[6] MSG

It is withstanding the forceful tides of temptation and lust. This is why protecting your integrity is incredibly more important than you may realize. For integrity, like innocence, once lost, may be gone forever. Are you behaving as a man in the same manner you want your children to? Stand fast and do all that you can to protect the quality, character, and integrity that you have contended so hard to establish.

Lack of integrity—or worse, the unwillingness to address it—has long-lasting repercussions that will affect people other then yourself. You can relocate, and it will follow you. You can change professions, acquire a new education or training, but it will still haunt you. Lack of integrity is a scourge for which there is only one cure: the act of being purposeful in becoming a man of integrity, no matter the cost.

Philanthropist W. Clement Stone said this, and it rings true, "Have the courage to say no. Have the courage to face the truth. Do the right thing because it is right. These are the magic keys to living your life with integrity."[7] Being a man is about making the difficult, yet ultimately, proper choices.

### The Integrity Equation

Telling the truth isn't enough. It is necessary of course, but that is only a part of the integrity equation. As a man, your actions, thoughts, and intentions need to mirror what you speak. Every effort you make without the other components is meaningless otherwise. The equation is rather simple, as is the answer. The practical application is where we fall short. I am not talking about the occasional misstep. I am talking about the negative and habitual patterns in your life. Here is the equation:

$$Truth + Actions + Intentions + Accountability = Integrity$$

The scriptures put it like this:

"The integrity of the honest keeps them on track; the deviousness of crooks brings them to ruin."

Proverbs 11:3[8] MSG

"My lips will not speak unjustly,
Nor will my tongue utter deceit.
Far be it from me that I should admit you are right [in your accusations against me];
Until I die, I will not remove my integrity from me.
I hold fast my uprightness *and* my right standing with God and I will not let them go;
My heart does not reproach me for any of my days."

Job 27:4-6[9] AMP

Right now, your inner dialogue must sound something like this: "I read the equation and see what the Bible says, but how does that apply to my life?" Here's a series of questions to ask yourself:

Are you the kind of gentleman whose word is worthless? When you make someone a promise do you frequently, if not always, break it?

Can people trust that your word is your bond? When you make a commitment, do you follow through or "forget" when it isn't convenient for you?

As a man, you, and the strength of your word, are considered to be one and the same. If you have the particular penchant to seldom follow through when you say you will, that speaks directly to how people see you, and the value that you place upon yourself and others as well.

It is all up to you. You have the power to change the trajectory of your life. Remember, slow change is still change. This isn't a sprint, it's a marathon. Rome wasn't built in a day, and it is foolhardy to think that these changes will set in overnight. Moreover, this is something that will take a lot longer for the people in your life to recognize. Make the change to better yourself. No one else can do it for you.

I am not just trying to piss in your Corn Flakes here guys. A more accurate example is this: You know those old horror movies from back in the day? There would often be a crazy mad scientist that was overly confident in what he had discovered. He would be the one to try the experimental operation or drink the magic elixir to see if it works.

Well, I am that mad scientist.

Trust me when I tell you that I have screwed up, and humiliated myself more often than not. Comedian Martin Lawrence said it best, "I'm most proud of the blessings that God has bestowed upon me, in my life. He's given me the vision to truly see that you can fall down, but you can still get back up. Hopefully I'll learn from my mistakes and have the opportunity to strengthen and improve the next thing I do."[10]

All men have stumbled. The greatest of men, usually have the greatest of falls. Look no further than Abraham Lincoln, who many believe to be the finest President the United States ever had. His record of failing is unequivocally superior to most men, but he learned from his mistakes and kept moving forward. It isn't the successes that define us and help us cultivate our integrity. It is the face down in the dirt, agonizing, soul crushing times when we have our asses handed to us that define our integrity and the truest measure of the man you are. President Dwight "Ike" Eisenhower puts it this way:

"The supreme quality for leadership is unquestionably integrity. Without it, no real success is possible, no matter whether it is on a section gang, a football field, in an army, or in an office."[11]

54

# Chapter 4
## Work Ethic And the Fruits of Labor

**work ethic / *noun* /** a belief in the moral benefit and importance of work and its inherent ability to strengthen character.[1]

**fruits of labor / *noun* /** the results of one's work.[2]

Having a strong work ethic is something that has been diminishing in many men in recent years, at an alarming rate. As a young man, the importance of working was stressed to me in a very concrete way. Having grandparents that lived through the Great Depression instilled something in my parents that seems to have eluded a vast majority of people in the generations that followed. The Bible says this on the subject:

"Don't you remember the rule we had when we lived with you? "If you don't work, you don't eat." And now we're getting reports that a bunch of lazy good-for-nothings are taking advantage of you. This must not be tolerated. We command them to get to work immediately—no excuses, no arguments—and earn their own keep. Friends, don't slack off in doing your duty."

2 Thessalonians 3:10-13[3] MSG

The ethics of work is an interesting philosophical concept to ponder. The idea that working, devotion to it, and that it is something that one should think on, is rather interesting. Yet this notion escapes so many men. Don't solely take my word on it. Here are a few quotes from some gentlemen you may have heard of before. I have chosen men who have had significant achievements in their lives. *Note: I didn't say that they were significant—their achievements were.* I believe that greatness lies just beneath the surface of all. The question is are you going to do the work that is required to mine and refine yourself to accomplish extraordinary things?

"I've viewed myself as slightly above average in talent. And where I excel is ridiculous, sickening work ethic."[4] –Will Smith

"The three great essentials to achieve anything worth while are: Hard work, Stick-to-itiveness, and Common sense."[5]     – Thomas A. Edison

"All life demands struggle. Those who have everything given to them become lazy, selfish, and insensitive to the real values of life. The very striving and hard work that we so constantly try to avoid is the major building block in the person we are today."[6]     – Pope Paul VI

I got my first job at thirteen. I worked with my dad. He was an auto body repairman, and heavy collision technician. (*Talk about a damn hard profession.*) A friend of his owned a body shop, so he would hustle on the weekends and evenings to earn some extra cash for the family. Dad, got me the hook up to be the janitor and porter. I was excited because it was my first steps into manhood. Well, that and the fact that I could buy more music and comic books. I think my folks were proud of me, and as I recall, I was the only one of my friends at the time with a job. It was an honest to God *job*. I punched a time card. I got a paycheck every two weeks and everything. I had officially entered the workforce!

That's where my excitement started and ended. I realized quickly, that getting a job actually means you have to work. My boss didn't just give me those checks for shits and giggles. Along the way as I swept, scrubbed, and cleaned I was beginning to learn the value of work. At the end of the day, I surveyed the shop, showroom, office, and bathroom I thought, "Hey it looks pretty good. I did that. Look at what I did!" The satisfaction that I got in my tweenage heart was an emotion the likes I had not experienced before. I can only imagine that's how Tom Hanks felt in *Castaway* when he made fire.

My responsibilities increased throughout the years, and I was taught more and more about how to repair cars. They showed me how to buff out scratches, pull out dents, mix bondo, remove parts from the vehicles, and even a few lessons in painting, but those never really took. When I turned sixteen and my senior year of high school started, I had the realization that this wasn't what I wanted to do with my life. So I got a job at a men's clothing store. It was a different kind of work entirely, but work nonetheless. I look back on those days at Waller Brothers Body & Paint Inc. with great fondness, even if I was too immature to appreciate them at the time. They were foundational in my understanding of what hard work is, and contrary to popular belief, work is not a dirty word. *(Pun intended.)*

Those late evenings, and early Saturday mornings, taught me a great deal. While many of my friends were out partying and goofing off, I was taking out trash, replacing those piss-stenched urinal cakes, and getting dirtier than a pig in mud. I began to appreciate what I used my paychecks to purchase. I had to think really hard, was whatever I wanted to buy worth all the effort that I expelled at my job? It really put things into perspective for me. I couldn't just go and ask my parents for money for things anymore.

Where did this whole ethic of work philosophy begin? Who was the originator of work ethic, and more importantly what do they have to say about it? I'm glad you asked. Of course it is from the Creator. From Genesis the Bible catalogues the lengths He went through to create our world. After He created it all, and chilled for a spell. He made man. God saw that it was proper and necessary that Adam work.

"God took the Man and set him down in the Garden of Eden to work the ground and keep it in order."

Genesis 2:15[7] MSG

This was incredibly important for two reasons. First, God understood that His creation, specifically The Garden of Eden, needed to be maintained. Second, Adam needed something to do. The Almighty created Adam with a purpose, to give reason to his life. In other words, God didn't just want Adam sitting on his "duff in the buff." Work is crucial for us men, to give our life structure, and meaning. Have you ever noticed that when most men retire, they start to become a bit unsettled and uneasy? They look for any kind of task or job to put their hands to, this is to distract and occupy them from the function that their career had given them. Upon further investigation of the Scriptures we discover that work does have a reward:

"Whatever you do [whatever your task may be], work from the soul [that is, put in your very best effort], as [something done] for the Lord and not for men, knowing [with all certainty] that it is from the Lord [not from men] that you will receive the inheritance which is your [greatest] reward. It is the Lord Christ whom you [actually] serve."

Colossians 3:23-24[8] AMP

Whether you are spiritually-minded or not, what we discover here is that there is a reward for our work. This verse is talking specifically about the inheritance of eternal life, but it should be duly noted that work has rewards in the physical sense also. The salary we earn from our jobs forwards us the opportunity to establish our household and provide for our family. This is something that, when carefully considered, goes way beyond some numbers and decimals on a little piece of paper we call a paycheck.

### Numbers Don't Lie

I love statistics. I devour them as quickly as I can find them. There are many reasons why, but one particularly: Statistics have no agenda. No motivation to choose a side or to be partial. They present no slant or spin. They are nondiscriminatory in their very nature. They are facts, the stone cold truth. They are a tool. Nothing more, nothing less.

As I have been researching for this chapter, I was curious to see if what I observed was really the lack of work ethic, or was just a fanciful whim, a veritable rabbit hole I was being lured down. So I searched, and confirmed with a few locations that I consider to be reputable, in order to verify for myself. What I found was actually worse than I had initially anticipated.

I began with the U.S. Census Bureau, as I trust that most people would view them as a non-bias, accurate resource. I found this from a census report released in November of 2011, the most recent as of writing this. Their findings were as followed, "Between 2005 and

2011, the proportion of young adults living in their parents' home increased, according to the U.S. Census Bureau. The percentage of men age 25 to 34 living in the home of their parents rose from 14 percent in 2005 to 19 percent in 2011 and from 8 percent to 10 percent over the period for women."[9]

Next, I visited Pew Research, another trusted organization. Richard Fry reported these statistics from his article in May of 2016, "In 2014, for the first time in more than 130 years, adults ages 18 to 34 were slightly more likely to be living in their parents' home than they were to be living with a spouse or partner in their own household."[10]

Fry breaks these statistics down into manageable categories to differentiate between the groups, "By 2014, 31.6% of young adults were living with a spouse or partner in their own household, below the share living in the home of their parent(s) (32.1%). Some 14% of young adults were heading up a household in which they lived alone, were a single parent or lived with one or more roommates. The remaining 22% lived in the home of another family member (such as a grandparent, in-law or sibling), a non-relative, or in group quarters (college dormitories fall into this category)."[10]

I found this to be very interesting, and then I thought, "Is this something unique to our current predicament in history?" Actually, it isn't. According to Fry, in this same article he reveals, "It's worth noting that the overall share of young adults living with their parents was not at a record high in 2014. This arrangement peaked around 1940, when about 35% of the nation's 18- to 34-year-olds lived with mom and/or dad (compared with 32% in 2014).[10] Now this is very telling indeed. Essentially, this is saying that more young people are living at home with their parents, since the time between The Great Depression and World War II. More accurately, men, by and large, are the ones who appear to be staying at home in greater numbers than women.

My next question was, "Why are these numbers increasing?" In December of 2014, New York Times reporter Amanda Cox wrote an article entitled, "The Rise of Men Who Don't Work, and What They Do Instead," Cox found data that lead her to the same questions I had. Cox stated, "In the late 1960s, almost all men between the ages of 25 and 54 went to work. Only about 5 out of every 100 did not have a job in any given week. By 2000, this figure had more than doubled, to 11 out of every 100 men. This year, it's 16. (People in the military, prison and institutions are excluded from these figures.)"[11]

I tried to come to some sort of deduction that could explain this phenomenon. I wanted to nail down specific reasons why, and I found two: a lack of motivation, and a sense of entitlement coupled with narcissism. Time magazine addressed this issue of lack of motivation with an article published in November of 2014, "2 in 5 Young Americans Don't Want a Job." Author Justin Worland writes, "Nearly 40% of people in the United States ages 16 to 24 say that they don't want a job, accounting for a sizable portion of the 92 million Americans who are currently outside the labor force, according to a new analysis of labor statistics.[12]

Another article, published in Time magazine from Joel Stein in May of 2013, offers a contextual synopsis of what we have been discussing these past few pages. "The incidence of narcissistic personality disorder is nearly three times as high for people in their 20s as for the generation that's now 65 or older, according to the National Institutes of Health; 58% more college students scored higher on a narcissism scale in 2009 than in 1982. Millennials got so many participation trophies growing up that a recent study showed that 40% believe they should be promoted every two years, regardless of performance. They are fame-obsessed: three times as many middle school girls want to grow up to be a personal assistant to a famous person as want to be a Senator, according to a 2007 survey; four times as many would pick the assistant job over CEO of a major corporation. They're so convinced of their own greatness that the National Study of Youth and Religion found the guiding morality of 60% of millennials in any situation is that they'll just be able to feel what's right. Their development is stunted: more people ages 18 to 29 live with their parents than with a spouse, according to the 2012 Clark University Poll of Emerging Adults. And they are lazy. In 1992, the nonprofit Families and Work Institute reported that 80% of people under 23 wanted to one day have a job with greater responsibility; 10 years later, only 60% did."[13]

### Earning Your Fruits

I acknowledge that this was not an exhaustive study covering the topic of decrease in work ethic, nor was it intended to be. The deeper I dove into the subject, the more I realized there was a never-ending list of resources and studies pointing in this general direction. However, numbers are just numbers and without making them personal or putting flesh on the statistical bones as it were, it is hard to put these figures into perspective in our life. As I learned, I attempted to evaluate, not only myself, but many of my friends and family members also.

As I began to look at my life and the lives of my friends and family, that is when it hit me that the above sources I quoted aren't wrong. The one aspect that they don't capture however, nor can they, is the individual circumstances that have caused these predicaments. Some of my friends had gotten divorced and had to move back home, some for a longer period of time then others. A few are pursuing Master's and Doctorate degrees. Many are buried under a mound of student loan debt, and if I am being honest, I am very doubtful they will ever be able to climb out from under. There are a few that have issues preventing them from working or going to school, such as mental or physical limitations. On the other hand, the overwhelming majority of them really have nothing preventing them from gainful and meaningful employment.

I'm sure you are familiar with the saying "Give a man a fish and he will eat for a day. Teach a man how to fish, and he will eat for a lifetime." I fear we have stopped teaching the value of work, and settled for the easier choice of just giving into people's demands with no sustainable responsibility required of them.

Linebacker James Harrison, said on his Instagram page in 2015, "I came home to find out that my boys received two trophies for nothing, participation trophies! While I am very proud of my boys for everything they do and will encourage them till the day I die, these trophies will be given back until they EARN a real trophy. I'm sorry I'm not sorry for believing that everything in life should be earned and I'm not about to raise two boys to be men by making them believe that they are entitled to something just because they tried their best...cause sometimes your best is not enough, and that should drive you to want to do better...not cry and whine until somebody gives you something to shut u up and keep you happy."[14] My hat's off to Mr. Harrison. His very matter-of-fact statement sums up what this chapter is about. The Bible puts it in these terms:

> "Train up a child in the way he should go [teaching him to seek God's wisdom and will for his abilities and talents], Even when he is old he will not depart from it."
>
> Proverbs 22:6[15] AMP

Do you have a strong work ethic? Have you been responsible instilling solid work ethic into those placed under your charge? Have we taken for granted the men in our life who have attempted to teach us the ethics and importance of work? Are we trying to do the very minimum, just eking by in life? Television host Mike Rowe says, "We've waged war on work. We have collectively agreed, stupidly, that work is the enemy." [16] This is quite an indictment coming from a man who has made a living jumping head first grinning into every kind of disgusting filth you can possibly imagine.

Educator Booker T. Washington said, "Nothing ever comes to one, that is worth having, except as a result of hard work."[17] Statesman Colin Powell puts it, "There are no secrets to success. It is the result of preparation, hard work, and learning from failure."[18] Thomas Edison, shed light on work ethic by noting, "What you are, will show in what you do."[19]

No matter the current trend, there is no substitute for hard work. Just as you judge a tree by its fruits, so men are judged by their quality, character, integrity, and work ethic. The more you try to ignore or shirk this responsibility, the more you only hurt yourself.

Many have desires to follow their dreams, turning their passions and hobbies into a paying reality. Don't get me wrong. Following your dreams is important, but you have to work to bring them to fruition, and have a legal means of paying the bills and putting food on your table in the interim.

I always chuckle when I hear people make comments like, "I can't work a full time job and pursue my passion." I'm not sure there is any other way to do it, honestly. It is the struggle, the ability to appreciate the challenges it took to nurture and develop your talent, and then watch it take root and grow, that, my friend, is the true reward of your hard work. The blessing is found in being able to look back and see where you started from, what it took to get you there, and then enjoying the fruits of your labor. It's like this:

> **"Those who work their land will have abundant food,
> but those who chase fantasies have no sense."**

Proverbs 12:11[20 NIV]

I respect songwriters, especially lyricists. Some of my favorite songwriters are Bob Dylan, Johnny Cash, Prince, Robbie Robertson, Adam Duritz, Bruce Springsteen, and Warren Zevon. Why do I bring this up? I think a lot of people will listen to songs and not for the slightest moment consider the actual words. The years of life and pain it took to create the experiences to be able to articulate the lyrical message. The struggles, and circumstances that compelled someone to write something that so personally effected them, that they had no choice but to put pen to paper, and speak directly to the listener, in the format of a three-and-a-half-minute Rock and Roll song.

Comedian Kevin Hart spoke about work ethic in this way, "Everybody wants to be famous, but nobody wants to do the work. I live by that. You grind hard so you can play hard. At the end of the day, you put all the work in, and eventually it'll pay off. It could be in a year, it could be in 30 years. Eventually, your hard work will pay off.[21]

It is here that I must warn you of something. We all want to enjoy the good fruits from labor. To see and take part of that in which we have cultivated from the sweat of our brow. It is the law of the harvest: You reap what you sow.

Be that as it may, just as you can enjoy fantastic fruits with the positive rewards that come from having a solid work ethic, it is also possible that you have horrible fruits from a flimsy or non-existent work ethic. It is truly a two-way street. As we see in this example of a horrible work ethic and the fruits thereof:

> "One day I walked by the field of an old lazybones,
> and then passed the vineyard of a lout;
> They were overgrown with weeds,
> thick with thistles, all the fences broken down.
> I took a long look and pondered what I saw;
> the fields preached me a sermon and I listened:
> "A nap here, a nap there, a day off here, a day off there,
> sit back, take it easy—do you know what comes next?
> Just this: You can look forward to a dirt-poor life,
> with poverty as your permanent houseguest!"

Proverbs 24:30-34 22 MSG

The author of this Proverb was able to see how a lack of work ethic and motivation leads to ruin, but also warns that doing nothing yields the same results. That a once beautiful and pristine vineyard had been laid to waste as a result of poor work ethic from some "old Lazybones." This demonstrates the contrast in fruits of labor. Work ethic and the fruits of your labor are joined at the hip. Good work ethic produces good fruits: spiritually, emotionally, physically, and monetarily. The other side of that coin is that poor work ethic produces poor results. The choice is yours.

Fellas, don't hate on, or be envious of someone who has worked hard to achieve a level of success. Those people, generally speaking, saw what they wanted to accomplish, figured out how to do so, and then executed the plan they formulated. Just because they have some things you want, but don't have, that doesn't make THEM bad, it makes YOU jealous.

Although the character of Rocky Balboa is a figment of Sylvester Stallone's imagination, he has been an engine of motivation and encouragement to millions of people, for several generations. This speech specifically, is one of the most prolific and powerful throughout the entire Rocky saga. As I close this chapter, allow these words to sink in.

"You ain't gonna believe this, but you used to fit right here. I'd hold you up to say to your mother, "This kid's gonna be the best kid in the world. This kid's gonna be somebody better than anybody I ever knew." And you grew up good and wonderful. It was great just watching you, every day was like a privilege. Then the time come for you to be your own man and take on the world, and you did. But somewhere along the line, you changed. You stopped being you. You let people stick a finger in your face and tell you you're no good. And when things got hard, you started looking for something to blame, like a big shadow.

Let me tell you something you already know. The world ain't all sunshine and rainbows. It's a very mean and nasty place and I don't care how tough you are it will beat you to your knees and keep you there permanently if you let it. You, me, or nobody is gonna hit as hard as life. But it ain't about how hard ya hit. It's about how hard you can get hit and keep moving forward. How much you can take and keep moving forward. That's how winning is done! Now if you know what you're worth then go out and get what you're worth. But ya gotta be willing to take the hits, and not pointing fingers saying you ain't where you wanna be because of him, or her, or anybody! Cowards do that and that ain't you! You're better than that!

I'm always gonna love you no matter what. No matter what happens. You're my son and you're my blood. You're the best thing in my life. But until you start believing in yourself, ya ain't gonna have a life."[23]

# Chapter 5
## Wisdom

**wisdom** / *noun* / "the quality or state of being wise; knowledge of what is true or right coupled with just judgment as to action; sagacity, discernment, or insight."[1]

"The [reverent] fear of the Lord [that is, worshiping Him and regarding Him as truly awesome] is the beginning *and* the preeminent part of knowledge [its starting point and its essence]; *But arrogant* fools despise [skillful and godly] wisdom and instruction *and* self-discipline."

Proverbs 1:7 [2] AMP

In order to comprehend wisdom, you must first properly be aware of the fear of the Lord. This is often a confusing subject, which is why I wanted to address it. You may know that the Bible wasn't initially written in English. Scholars have been able to study the original Hebraic text in which portions of it was written. The Hebrew language is a much richer and descriptive language than most contemporary ones, and the modern translations of these ancient words often do not serve us well. Such is the case we have here. "Fear" in this portion of scripture can be defined as meaning reverence, respect, and wonder. So you can literally read the first section of the verse like this, "Having respect for the Lord." Another interesting tidbit here is the word "beginning." One word I would include in the scripture is "principle." So how about we put them together? "Having respect for the Lord is the principle component of obtaining wisdom."

Additionally, take note of the fool, and his rejection of wisdom. I found this commentary very interesting in reference to this verse, "In Proverbs various kinds of fools are discussed including those who are closed-minded, over-confident, and reject instruction and correction—the unteachable; those who lack spiritual insight—the spiritually blind; and those who are flippant, hardened, and who deliberately choose to reject God and wisdom—the arrogant."[2] I mention this because I want you to have a wide breath and depth in your understanding as to what we are discussing here. Please don't allow close-minded, over-confident, and unteachable mindsets to rob you of wisdom's lessons.

Most of us make boneheaded mistakes, and often end up scratching our head wondering why. I don't mean the occasional screw up—I am talking about the consistent (and arguably deliberate) manner in which we sabotage our lives. I've picked this up somewhere along the way: "To learn from your mistakes is wisdom. To learn from someone else's mistakes, is genius." This is a trustworthy saying that has served me well. Albert Einstein said, "The difference between stupidity and genius is that genius has its limits."[3] My hope is that we can gain wisdom, and learn how to practically apply it in our lives.

## Brilliant Idiots

Wisdom mustn't be confused with knowledge. We see that word knowledge is defined as, "acquaintance with facts, truths, or principles, as from study or investigation; general erudition."[4] Knowledge has to do with the acquaintance or familiarity of facts and truth. Albeit important, knowledge is not by definition comprised of the same ingredients as wisdom. Our society is littered with giants of academia, and those who pursue higher education to various ends. Simply enrolling into school isn't the lone qualifier for acquiring wisdom.

Wisdom is also not to be confused with information. Information by definition means, "knowledge communicated or received concerning a particular fact or circumstance; news."[5] Information as we understand, is knowledge about one item or issue. It is not necessarily a multitude of items, although one may certainly possess information about a plethora of subjects. It is important to have information so you can be wise, yet wisdom does not reside solely in information's neighborhood.

Logic is another flawed substitute for wisdom. Logic defined is, "the science that investigates the principles governing correct or reliable inference."[6] This is the scientific evaluation of examining different items to determine whether or not reason can be applied in conjunction to a subject using principles of philosophy and mathematics. Logic is a most useful weapon to have in your arsenal. The ability to apply reason, and deduction, to determine the outcome of any given occasion whether it will be successful or not is a priceless and crucial part of the development of wisdom. Yet logic is not wisdom in and of itself; it is merely only one color in wisdom's rainbow pallet.

Knowledge, information, and logic all lend a hand in the process of being wise, and the practical application of wisdom in ones life, but those factors themselves do not translate specifically to wisdom. There is a weightiness and responsibility that one is required to bear in the relentless pursuit of wisdom. Ancient Chinese philosopher Confucius said, "By three methods we may learn wisdom: First, by reflection, which is noblest; Second, by imitation, which is easiest; and third by experience, which is the bitterest."[7] The bitter experience Confucius refers to is the smack down that life readily dishes out to those with enough gravitas to tempt its fate. Some people, like myself, have to learn things the hard way.

You finally get the revelation of the value of these lessons and see how they are relevant to your life as you continue on your quest. President Calvin Coolidge observed, "Knowledge comes, but wisdom lingers. It may not be difficult to store up in the mind a vast quantity of facts within a comparatively short time, but the ability to form judgments requires the severe discipline of hard work and the tempering heat of experience and maturity."[8]

I was once engaged, and I can now say this with a rational heart: we were just wrong for each other. No finger pointing, no blame assessed. Had I been a little wiser, and a tad more astute, I would have detected that when we first met. But this was a major part of my process in developing wisdom when it comes to relationships.

The first thing that should have tipped me off was that my friends and family couldn't stand her. Most of them didn't tell me directly, but near the end, a couple did. The invites to hang out became fewer and fewer the longer we were together. Not only were invites rarely extended, but there were less people accepting our offers in return. One on one, my friends and family still called and spent time with me, but they didn't really like when we would come to events as a couple. That should have been an obvious clue. The fact that the ones who loved me the most and were closest to me didn't approve should have been a clarion call.

Another red flag I missed, was that we didn't see eye to eye on political ideologies or societal morals. Not that everyone has to, or will at all times, but there needs to be a commonality in these areas. In a marriage type relationship, with the possibility of raising children, this becomes all the more important. It wasn't as much of an issue when we first met, but it really became apparent after we got engaged, when there was a presidential election, and the dreaded Y2K kerfuffle (*Google it if you don't know*). Our approaches were vastly different, and that lead to tension, specifically within our families at large.

About the only thing we agreed on, was the physical. In nearly every other department we were absolutely incompatible, but in this area, we had an accord. What I wasn't wise enough to comprehend at the time was that the physical part of a relationship ratio is comprised of around ten percent, while all the other components (spiritual, financial, and emotional) are ninety. I got it all backwards, I thought getting off was more important than getting along.

I do not regret that relationship, or any I've had since. They have all taught me a great deal about myself and whom I wanted to be with. I learned that just because there is an overabundance of sexual satisfaction, that doesn't necessarily equate to relational fulfillment. I learned that even the most beautiful woman, will be overwhelmingly repugnant, if her physique doesn't mirror what her heart is comprised of. I learned that we all get old, gray, and saggy, and that if there isn't anything else in the relationship going on, other than just sex, you are doomed for a lonely life. I learned that if you have to stretch your monetary means in order to get her, you will go well beyond those same means to keep her.

I have dated a lot of women. This is a fact, which now that I am a little bit older, and a wee bit wiser (*hopefully*). I look back upon in contempt. Many of us are lead to believe that the more sexual conquests we have, they will inevitably help lead us into manhood. I used to think that, too. The best thing I took away from my many excursion through the murky, and shallow waters of the dating pool, is what I did not want. I was able to taste and see what was unappealing to me, so that when I did see what I wanted it was made all the more clearer. This is how the process works:

> "When I was a boy at my father's knee,
> the pride and joy of my mother,
> He would sit me down and drill me:
> "Take this to heart. Do what I tell you—live!
> Sell everything and buy Wisdom! Forage for Understanding!
> Don't forget one word! Don't deviate an inch!
> Never walk away from Wisdom—she guards your life;
> love her—she keeps her eye on you.
> Above all and before all, do this: Get Wisdom!
> Write this at the top of your list: Get Understanding!
> Throw your arms around her—believe me, you won't regret it;

never let her go—she'll make your life glorious.
She'll garland your life with grace,
she'll festoon your days with beauty."

Proverbs 4:6-9 [9] MSG


**Uncommon Sense**

Unfortunately, our I.Q.'s have little to do with wisdom. Wisdom, or
lack thereof, is acknowledged in the wake of our decisions. I am
rarely seeing the concept of common sense applied in our daily lives.
As a child, I would always hear my parents say, "Use your common
sense!" As I made my way through life, situations would arise with
my friends, co-workers, or family members. I would look at the
aftermath of the decisions they made. I would frequently say to
myself *(and to them personally on occasion)*, "Damn! Where was
your commonsense on that one?"


What I have discovered is that common sense really isn't as common
as we would like to think. I took for granted that everyone was raised
to learn what common sense was, and more importantly, how to use
it. Now, before you just dismiss this notion, how about we examine
it a little further? Let's take a look at the definition:


**common sense** / *noun* / sound practical judgment that is
independent of specialized knowledge, training, or the like; normal
native intelligence.[10]

Wisdom and common sense are kissing cousins; two sides of the same coin. Call it six, or half a dozen, they are for all intents and purposes, garments cut from the same cloth. Rapper Nas says, "With age comes common sense and wisdom."[11] What we currently have in our culture is a deficit in common sense. What do I mean by this? I'm glad you asked.

Here are a few things I've noticed in regards to an apparent lack of wisdom and common sense. What is your email address? Is it ProfessionalMan@trustworthyperson.com? Or is it BigPimpin@suchandsuch.com? Or maybe it is BootyGrabber1@whatever.com? Whenever I receive emails and I see the address, I automatically dismiss the crazy ones. Want to know why? Because you only get one chance to make a first impression.

Another example is a person's appearance. Now don't get me wrong, I usually choose comfort over style. Be that as it may, there are those occasions where one needs to dress appropriately. For instance: funerals, weddings, and any other formal proceedings. I used to conduct interviews in several of my past positions, and one of the first things that I took note of was the manner in which someone presented themself. If an applicant showed up wearing attire that was suitable for the job they were seeking, I was inclined to be more interested in what they had to say.

Men, when you are trying to achieve something great in your life, you have to make an effort that surpasses what you ordinarily exhibit.

One must consider the fact that every action has an equal and opposite reaction. It is true in everything. If you apply wisdom and common sense when making decisions, you will avoid much turmoil. It really is quite remarkable. Comedian Josh Billings, said, "Common sense is the knack of seeing things as they are, and doing things as they ought to be done."[12]

### Go With Your Gut

I am sure at this point you are thinking of past, and even present situations, where you can begin to see how using wisdom can change the outcome for your best interest. I think the question we need to consider asking ourselves is, "how is it possible moving forward to consistently apply wisdom in our lives?" Here are a few recommendations:

### 1. Go with your gut.

Ever heard anyone say, "I should've listen to my gut?" Well there is actually a scientific reasoning behind this. Carlin Flora wrote this in a June 2016 article appearing in Psychology Today, "Intuitions, or gut feelings, are sudden, strong judgements whose origin we can't immediately explain. Although they seem to emerge from an obscure inner force, they actually begin with a perception of something outside—a facial expression, a tone of voice, a visual inconsistency so fleeting you're not even aware you noticed. Think of them as a rapid cognition or condensed reasoning that takes advantage of the brains built-in shortcuts. Or think of intuition as an unconscious associative process."

Flora went on to say, :The best explanation psychologists now offer is that intuition is a mental matching game. The brain takes in a situation, does a very quick search of its files, and then finds its best analogue among the stored sprawl of memories and knowledge. Based on that analogy, you ascribe meaning to the situation in front of you." 13

I like to say, "The gut knows." I have found when I ignore my gut, I usually ended up regretting it in the long run. Having the foresight to trust your gut, lends to cultivating wisdom, and common sense in your life. Leonardo da Vinci was quoted saying, "Common Sense is that which judges the things given to it by other senses."14

## 2. Study.

I love history. I read and watch any material pertaining to historical events, and individuals, that I can. I am a firm believer that history does nothing but repeat itself. If you want to accurately predict the future, just look at the past.

One primary source I find helps me retain wisdom is the Bible. All scriptures have stories and parables that contain pearls of wisdom, but two books in particular, Proverbs and James, are specifically noted for their exhaustive content of wisdom. Allow me to share a few of my favorites with you:

> "And here's why: God gives out Wisdom free,
> is plainspoken in Knowledge and Understanding.
> He's a rich mine of Common Sense for those who live well,
> a personal bodyguard to the candid and sincere.
> He keeps his eye on all who live honestly,
> and pays special attention to his loyally committed ones"
> Proverbs 2:6-8[15] AMP

> "The wise accumulate wisdom; fools get stupider by the day."
> Proverbs 14:24[15] AMP

> "If you think you know it all, you're a fool for sure; real survivors
> learn wisdom from others."
> Proverbs 28:26[15] AMP

> "If any of you lacks wisdom, you should ask God, who gives
> generously to all without finding fault, and it will be given to you."
> James 1:5[16] NIV

"Who is wise and understanding among you? Let them show it by their good life, by deeds done in the humility that comes from wisdom."
James 3:13[16] NIV

## 3. Remain Watchful.

Watch people, places, and things. Not in a creep

y, stalker-ish way, but more akin to an exercise in an anthropological study. Watching people screw up is one of the most painless and valuable methods for gaining wisdom I know of. If you take a long enough look around, you will observe someone doing something that you will end up saying to yourself. "WOW. I am *not* going to do that." You see, that right there is wisdom. Entertainer Will Rogers said, "There are three kinds of men. The one that learns by reading. The few who learn by observation. The rest of them have to pee on the electric fence for themselves."[17] Jesus himself said:

"Keep *actively* watching and praying that you may not come into temptation"

Matthew 26:41[18] AMP

## 4. Pray.

I know it may not seem deep, but I just converse with God. It is extremely easy to talk to Him. I speak to him just as I am speaking to anyone else. He doesn't care about using proper English or any of that rigid dogmatic nonsense. As a matter of fact, I speak to Him much in the same way I am speaking to you, and in our

84

conversations, I use the same verbiage and phrasing, with the cheesy humor to boot. He cares about what you care about and is eager to hear from you. We're encouraged to:


"Come near to God and he will come near to you."

James 4:8[19] NIV

No matter which combination of these components I use, prayer is always the one that is included. Much like everything in this book, it takes time to effectively see the desired results, but trust me it is worth it. No matter what any religious figure has told you or any theological ordinance may have lead you to believe, I assure you it is not as complex as you may think. He is as close as a whisper away.

At the end of the day, the below verse is one, in my opinion, that encompasses the qualities we should strive to emulate in our quest to obtaining wisdom. I would be remiss if I didn't bring this to your attention:


"But the wisdom from above is first pure [morally and spiritually undefiled], then peace-loving [courteous, considerate], gentle, reasonable [and willing to listen], full of compassion and good fruits. It is unwavering, without [self-righteous] hypocrisy [and self-serving guile]."

James 3:17[20] AMP

As I bring this chapter to a close, my greatest concern is that I have only marginally addressed the issue of wisdom. People have spent large portions of their lives and wealth in search of it. I shudder to think that I have managed to only narrowly scratched the surface. With that being said, allow me to leave you with a thought from one of our greatest contemporary philosophers.

"Stupid is as stupid does."[21]

— Forrest Gump

# Chapter 6
## Decisiveness

**decisiveness** / *adjective* / "1. having the power or quality of deciding; putting an end to controversy; crucial or most important: 2. characterized by or displaying no or little hesitation; resolute; determined"[1]

It is astonishing to me that men these days are so wishy-washy. Actor Clint Eastwood has gone on record saying, "We're really in a p*ssy generation. Everybody's walking on eggshells."[2] I have to say, Mr. Eastwood isn't wrong. I am consistently running into men who embody the namby-pamby mentality that is so pervasive in our culture. I am beginning to seriously question if the male gender is being deliberately bred into becoming a bunch of genetically engineered spineless crybabies.

I have a few theories for why this phenomenon is occurring which I will get into shortly. But I wanted to begin with this:

"A double minded man is unstable in all his ways."

James 1:8[3] KJV

This verse speaks directly to the heart of the issue we will discuss in this chapter. I have been encountering men from all different kinds of backgrounds, many of whom you would not assume would share any kind of commonality, but alas they do: It is the apparent inability to make a decision that bares any nuances of significance. More simply put, so many of us men are shirking our responsibility as the leaders we were intended to be. Remember, not every leader is a man, but every man is a leader. To someone you are a person in whom people will look to for guidance, and you cannot give it to them when you can not perform the most basic of tasks, which is making a decision. After all, indecision is the calling card of fools.

Just to clarify, I am not suggesting basic decisions like, what you're going to have for dinner, or what kind of cereal for breakfast. What I am referring to are decisions that carry weightiness to them. The kind of questions that when once presented, do need to be approached with careful consideration and thought intensely upon. Though not always easy to make, they do at some point demand that a decision must be reached. I see so many guys just putting things off on the back burner if you will, not being able or not wanting to make a commitment either way. Super Hero Vigilante Frank Castle, a.k.a. The Punisher, said, "No matter where you turn, there's a decision to be made. Life or death. Right or wrong. Regular or crunchy."[4]

**Miyagi's Wisdom**

*The Karate Kid* was a very influential movie to me in my youth. There's a lot of important life lessons in this film. It teaches respect, true character, how to stand up for yourself and others, and that there may come a time when proper defense will be needed in life. It demonstrated that a gentleman fights from the heart, and only engages in violence when it is absolutely necessary. One of the many exchanges that has always struck me as profound, was the conversation right before Mr. Miyagi agreed to teach Daniel-san karate. It goes a little something like this:

> **Miyagi**: Now, ready?
> **Daniel-san**: Yeah, I guess so.
> **Miyagi**: Daniel-san, must talk.
> **Miyagi**: Walk on road, hmm? Walk left side, safe. Walk right side, safe. Walk middle, sooner or later
> [*makes squish gesture*]
> **Miyagi**: get squish just like grape. Here, karate, same thing. Either you karate do "yes" or karate do "no." You karate do "guess so,"
> [*makes squish gesture*]
> **Miyagi**: just like grape. Understand?
> **Daniel-san**: Yeah, I understand.
> **Miyagi**: Now, ready?
> **Daniel-san**: Yeah, I'm ready.[5]

What Mr. Miyagi was teaching Daniel-san, was not only applicable to their situation, but it is unquestionably apropos to a man's regular daily life. Mr. Miyagi is telling Daniel-san that he needed to make a commitment and stick with it. Be decisive, follow through. This scripture makes it very apparent as to what manner in which man should approach all decisions:

"All you need to say is simply 'Yes' or 'No'; anything beyond this comes from the evil one."

Matthew 5:37[6] NIV

Just say yes or no. Most people would rather you answer them flat out, than have you hemming and hawing around, not being decisive or making a decision either way. I know when I need help; personally, I would prefer that when they can't, or if they don't want to, to be upfront and honest. It is just fine with me. I will assume that it is okay with most people as well. Actually, you are just being unappreciative of somebody's dilemma, not giving them a definitive answer. What you are really doing is causing frustration, because by being indecisive, you just wasted their time and are now making them search for other methods to accomplish the task at hand.

As you read the above scripture, you may have noticed it stated that being noncommittal is from "the evil one." You may be asking yourself, "How can that be?" Let me elaborate:

"For God is not the author of confusion, but of peace"

1 Corinthians 14:33[7] KJV

This verse explains it as matter-of-factly as possible. God is not the author of confusion. Those moments in life when you feel the most lost and bewildered, try to stop and think, "God is not behind this." How do I know? Because:

> "For I know the plans *and* thoughts that I have for you,' says the Lord, 'plans for peace *and* well-being and not for disaster to give you a future and a hope."
>
> Jeremiah 29:11[8 AMP]

The Almighty has plans and purposes for you, and He doesn't change His mind. His plans are for good, and not destructive ends. To bless, not curse. Part of being decisive is trusting and knowing that God has better things in store for you than you can even imagine. This is further supported by the following:

> "You watched me as I was being formed in utter seclusion,
> as I was woven together in the dark of the womb.
> You saw me before I was born.
> Every day of my life was recorded in your book.
> Every moment was laid out
> before a single day had passed.
> How precious are your thoughts about me, O God.
> They cannot be numbered!"
>
> Psalm 139:15-17[9 AMP]

Even the trials and tribulations we endure, are ultimately for our benefit. So how do we connect the dots here? We see that, as men, we are obligated to give an answer when life calls upon us. We see that procrastination is not from The Almighty. God does not create confusion. His intentions toward you are steadfast, and for your betterment. He knows which direction you should take before you even come to the forks in the road that are ahead of you. All we must do is ask Him. Plain and simple.

While you continue reading, keep this in mind. There is no time like the present. Writer Napoleon Hill recommends that, "The way to develop decisiveness is to start right where you are, with the very next question you face."[10]

### No Swayze, No Wayze

Revisiting James 1:8 from earlier in this chapter, we see that it doesn't pull any punches. Double mindedness causes us to be unstable in all that we do. We could label this kind of behavior as chronic indecisiveness. Philosopher William James explains, "There is no more miserable human being than one in whom nothing is habitual but indecision."[11] There is no ability to commit to a decision, whether right or wrong. No progress. No moving forward. Just a perpetually stagnant state of being.

It should be noted that there is a world of difference between taking some time to weigh all your options, verses postponing a decision all together. The decision-making process for men is generally internalized, while women are externalized. Just because you're not verbalizing your decision-making process in and of itself it not a bad thing. It is when the wheels stop turning and you quit the process entirely that problems occur. I have come to an understanding, that is truly tiring behavior, not only to the individual, but to those around them also. Philosopher Bertrand Russell elegantly puts it, "Nothing is so exhausting as indecision, and nothing is so futile."[12] However, this doesn't explain the inherent lack of being decisive, only illuminates it. I have observed a couple reasons I believe this is an issue amongst so many men.

## 1. Fear

Fear is one thing that will absolutely demolish a man, I've witnessed it stop them dead in their tracks. Actor Patrick Swayze said it best in the film *Point Break:* "Fear causes hesitation, and hesitation will cause your worst fears to come true."[13] Fear has such an incredibly strong grip on so many of us men. This is nothing to be ashamed of, it happens to the very best of us from time to time.

Pastor Charles Stanley has said, "Fear stifles our thinking and actions. It creates indecisiveness that results in stagnation. I have known talented people who procrastinate indefinitely rather than risk failure. Lost opportunities cause erosion of confidence, and the downward spiral begins."[14] If we can sincerely look into our hearts when these moments arise, we can begin to combat these fears. Fear can be turned into this acronym; False Evidence Appearing Real. President Franklin D. Roosevelt was famously noted for saying, "The only thing we have to fear is fear itself."[15]

We all have fears to face, so face your fears head on. If you must complete a task and you're afraid, do it afraid. What I've learned is, no matter the circumstance or situation, things usually don't end up as terrible in reality as they do in my mind. The only things in life you regret are the chances you didn't take. My friend, do not allow your fear to cripple you any longer.

## 2. Procrastination

Hockey Player Wayne Gretzky, once said, "Procrastination is one of the most common and deadliest of diseases and its toll on success and happiness is heavy."[16] When we put off making critical choices, we aren't solving any problems. However, we do create brand new ones. The scripture says:

"Don't put it off; do it now! Don't rest until you do."

Proverbs 6:4[17] NLT

Putting off the decision-making process does not relieve you from having to make a final decision, nor will it change what the

94

inevitable outcome will be. You cannot just continue to kick the can down the road, in the hopes that the situation will just go away, or rectify itself. President Abraham Lincoln said, "You cannot escape the responsibility of tomorrow by evading it today."[18] You have the ability to make a wise decision. I would say the question to ask yourself is: do you have the intestinal fortitude to pull that trigger? Look, I get it; certain decisions in life aren't easy. We may wish for the situation to resole itself, so we can just keep on keeping on with our daily routine. Sorry to be the one to burst your bubble, but that isn't how it works. And it's not in line with what being a man is about.

I can tell you one time in my life when procrastination would have been fatal. I used to weigh well over six hundred pounds. I was very sick, and my health was rapidly declining, mostly due to being overweight. It was recommended that I have a gastric bypass in order to help preserve what was left of my quality of life. After a heart to heart conversation with my dad, I decided to go ahead with the procedure. It took several months to arrange everything and to lose the required ten percent of my body weight on my own as a sign of good faith that I would continue to maintain a healthy lifestyle after the bypass. The entire procedure was scheduled to take about an hour and a half, and was to be performed laparoscopically. On the day of the surgery, just as I was saying goodbye to my family, the doctor came and said a few things to us. As she finished speaking, and left to get prepared, she turned and said, "Just to let you know, in case something unforeseen happens, I reserve the right to open your abdominal region, to perform the surgery."

"Oh" I said, Have you ever had to do that before?" I asked.

"No," she replied. "Don't worry I have done thousands of these surgeries and never had to open up anyone. I just tell you for precautionary reasons."

This was something that concerned me greatly and the primary reason I hesitated on getting this done in the past. I had known someone who, years before, had a gastric bypass using this method, and it was a long and painful recovery. I am kind of a wimp, so I never really considered this option for weight loss based solely on that fact. At any rate, guess who was the first patient my doctor had the unfortunate pleasure of having to perform the procedure that way?

You guessed it!

Once the operation began, the surgical team discovered that I had a congenital birth defect. It was a very serious and rare occurrence that may have been a contributing factor to my lifelong obesity. The operation took nearly eight hours, instead of the scheduled hour and a half. I ended up staying in the I.C.U. for eight days. During my time there, I caught pneumonia. My arms went numb because they were elevated above my head the entire length of the operation causing circulation issues. Afterwards, I had limited range of motion in both arms, and still do to this day. There was also an issue with a potential clot in the central artery in my left leg.

Additionally, I had an adverse reaction to the pain medication I was on and I began to have  hallucinations (*you will never experience terror as I did during one hallucination where Batman was battling with The Joker to stop him from stealing my soul*). Perhaps the most valuable thing that I learned, that I will pass along to you is this: never trust a fart while you're in the hospital.

I told you that story to say the doctor had to act quickly. She couldn't simply mull it over and think, "Maybe if I just stuff everything back in his gut, and staple him shut, his problem will eventually go away." No! That wasn't an option. I can honestly tell you that even after all the turmoil and the extensive recovery process, which included months of physical therapy. I am very appreciative that she acted decisively that day. My quality of life has improved drastically. I am literally two-thirds the man I used to be.

Actor Denzel Washington says this about procrastination, "I'd be more frightened by not using whatever abilities I'd been given. I'd be more frightened by procrastination and laziness." [19] The ability lies within you, to not only make a decision, but to make a good one at that. Decisiveness is the hallmark of a man of conviction.

### 3. Opinions and Approval

Maybe you don't want to offend anyone. That's admirable. Perhaps you are afraid of what others will think of you. At some point, you will upset someone no matter what you may say or do. That's just something that will eventually happen. You can't please everyone all the time, and if these feelings control you, it might be there is a deeper issue you may be struggling with. Here's some food for thought:

> "The fear of human opinion disables; trusting in God protects you from that."
> Proverbs 29:25 [20] MSG

> "For am I now seeking the approval of man, or of God? Or am I trying to please man? If I were still trying to please man, I would not be a servant of Christ."
> Galatians 1:10 [21] ESV

As we see in these two verses, being preoccupied with what others may think, should not be our primary concern. Our concentration should be devoted to pleasing God and doing what is right. We need to take our family, and true friend's opinions into consideration, however the reality is, that you will not always see eye to eye even with them. This strikes at the core of what being a decisive man is all about. We have our own thoughts and ideas—free will as it were—and when we subject that to others, a part of us dies, and we slowly lose the quality and character of who we are.

I hope that you can see this is not a license to dismiss all of those that may disagree with you. On the contrary, there is great wisdom that comes from seeking the advice of those we respect, and in whom have earned the right to speak into your life. Peripheral people have not paid their dues to have sway over you, so their opinion of you should not really matter. Those who you hold in esteem have been given that access, and their words do carry weight. But they can't make up your mind for you. The decision lies in your hands. You are responsible for YOUR success or failure, not anyone else's. Since the responsibility is all yours, opinions and approval must not stop you from making the hard choices in your life.

What I have discovered about other people's opinions is this: opinions are like armpits, everyone has a couple and they usually stink. Actor Terrence J said, "You can't take people's opinions personally. Usually what people say about it is a reflection of them own issues."[22] Businessman Les Brown stated, "Don't let someone else's opinion of you become your reality."[23] You are not captive to other's idiosyncrasies or hang-ups. The longest distance in the human experience is that from the heart, to the brain. The course that we plot in the decision making process, often ends up becoming a grueling journey. Don't allow other people's baggage to weigh you down on your quest. Whether it is fear, procrastination, or other people's opinions and approval that is prohibiting you from being a man of decisiveness, you can overcome it.

## Jesus' Lougee

As this chapter draws to an end, I want to leave you with these final thoughts. Men must not give into the fashions or frivolousness of the moments they occupy in history. Remember, decisiveness is a hallmark of a man of conviction, while indecision is the calling card of fools.

The final scripture I will use in this chapter is from Jesus himself. He is addressing the church of Laodicea in Revelation 3. Jesus admonishes them with this warning:

> "I know your deeds, that you are neither cold nor hot. I wish you were either one or the other! So, because you are lukewarm—neither hot nor cold—I am about to spit you out of my mouth."
> Revelation 3:15-16 [24] NIV

When Jesus is discussing these issues using terminology such as "neither hot or cold" and "lukewarm," he is directly confronting the issue of being indecisive. He preferred that they, as well as you and I, be decisive. Gentlemen, you must decide to no longer linger on the shores of procrastination.

"Do or Do not. There is no try."[25]
— Yoda

"Never half-ass two things. Whole-ass one thing."[26]
— Ron Swanson

# Chapter 7
## Benevolence

**benevolence** / *noun* / "1. desire to do good to others; goodwill; charitableness:
2. an act of kindness; a charitable gift."[1]

Thus far we have discussed changes throughout culture that have been attempting to neuter us men. However, the subject matter contained within this chapter is a bit different. We will be highlighting a quality which, whether by societal misconceptions or not, lack in many of us, regardless of gender.

A man whose heart is absent of benevolence, is one that is most sincerely impoverished. While a man may have laid held of many of the qualities we've discussed, without this crucial element, it is all for naught.

Are you concerned about people mistaking your kindness for weakness? Is your personal philosophy that you always have to look out for number one? When you engage in conversation, do you constantly have to have the last word? If you encounter someone whose opinion differs from yours, can you not relent in the debate until you have proven your point? These notions are part of the huge shift in our culture with regards to what true manliness is. The pendulum typically swings to one of two extremes, either embracing the consciousness of castration, or full-blown peacocking. Just in case you haven't figured it out yet, both of these are wrong.

So what are we talking about here? Basically it boils down to loving others above ourselves, or as I like to say, preferring others rather than oneself. That's a difficult pill to swallow. Sadly, I can speak from having great familiarity with this. When we talk about benevolence, the under current must be love. So many of us men have a hard time grasping what love is, how to receive, and more importantly, how to give love. The following passage is the greatest definition of love ever written. Let these simple words course through your heart as we move through this chapter and our quest:

"If I could speak all the languages of earth and of angels, but didn't love others, I would only be a noisy gong or a clanging cymbal. If I had the gift of prophecy, and if I understood all of God's secret plans and possessed all knowledge, and if I had such faith that I could move mountains, but didn't love others, I would be nothing. If I gave everything I have to the poor and even sacrificed my body, I could boast about it; but if I didn't love others, I would have gained nothing.
Love is patient and kind. Love is not jealous or boastful or proud or rude. It does not demand its own way. It is not irritable, and it keeps no record of being wronged. It does not rejoice about injustice but rejoices whenever the truth wins out. Love never gives up, never loses faith, is always hopeful, and endures through every circumstance.

Prophecy and speaking in unknown languages and special knowledge will become useless. But love will last forever! Now our knowledge is partial and incomplete, and even the gift of prophecy reveals only part of the whole picture!
But when the time of perfection comes, these partial things will become useless.
When I was a child, I spoke and thought and reasoned as a child. But when I grew up, I put away childish things. Now we see things imperfectly, like puzzling reflections in a mirror, but then we will see everything with perfect clarity. All that I know now is partial and incomplete, but then I will know everything completely, just as God now knows me completely.
Three things will last forever—faith, hope, and love—and the greatest of these is love."

1 Corinthians 13[2 NLT]


## The Pennyworth Model

The scriptures speak of benevolence, and the qualities thereof many times. The following verse in particular sums up the heart of one who is benevolent and the required discipline it takes to master such a concept. It's presented here in two different translations for us to mull over. The subtleties and distinctive nuances offer a comprehensive understanding into what the author was implying.


"Pure and genuine religion in the sight of God the Father means caring for orphans and widows in their distress and refusing to let the world corrupt you."
James 1:27[3 NLT]

"Anyone who sets himself up as "religious" by talking a good game

is self-deceived. This kind of religion is hot air and only hot air. Real religion, the kind that passes muster before God the Father, is this: Reach out to the homeless and loveless in their plight, and guard against corruption from the godless world."
James 1:26-27[4] MSG

What we should take away from these verses is that a man ought to show kindness to those of whom cannot repay it. As a man, when you engage in the act of benevolence, you are engaging God. Jesus himself said this:

"Then those 'sheep' are going to say, 'Master, what are you talking about? When did we ever see you hungry and feed you, thirsty and give you a drink? And when did we ever see you sick or in prison and come to you?' Then the King will say, 'I'm telling the solemn truth: Whenever you did one of these things to someone overlooked or ignored, that was me—you did it to me.'
"Then he will turn to the 'goats,' the ones on his left, and say, 'Get out, worthless goats! You're good for nothing but the fires of hell.
And why?
Because— I was hungry and you gave me no meal,
I was thirsty and you gave me no drink,
I was homeless and you gave me no bed,
I was shivering and you gave me no clothes,
Sick and in prison, and you never visited."
Matthew 25:39-43[5] MSG

In these verses, the true heart of God is made known to us. You may have heard it said before that, "A man is never as tall as when he stoops down to help someone." This is a trustworthy saying. Orphans, widows, the indigent, our neighbors, friends and family, the person in their car who has broken down on the side of the road. Your co-worker who may need a hand from time to time. Maybe the couple down at the end of your street that is retired and needs help shoveling the snow from their driveway. These are all people you have the tremendous pleasure of giving a benevolent hand to.

When I ponder examples of a true man of benevolence, there is one character in fiction that immediately comes to mind, Alfred Thaddeus Crane Pennyworth. For those of you unacquainted with Mr. Pennyworth, he is an integral part throughout the mythology of Batman. When young Bruce Wayne witnessed the murders of his parents Dr. Thomas and Martha Wayne, he became an orphan. Alfred Pennyworth was the Wayne family's trusted butler and he assumed the role of legal guardian to Master Wayne. In the mythology, Alfred became, not only Bruce's caretaker, but his teacher, mentor, legal advisor, co-conspirator of The Bat Man, and most consistent and loyal confidant.

One can only assume the enormity of this task. For starters, this man was charged with the care of the Wayne estate, assets, and all that entailed. More importantly, he accepted the responsibility to steward Dr. and Mrs. Wayne's most valuable possession, their only son. Now you could argue that Alfred had it made. He could live his life in the lap of luxury and spend his days plundering the treasure left for him to manage. He could have just thrown Bruce into some private boarding school, only dealing with him when it was absolutely necessary. Yet, he didn't. He raised and loved Bruce as his own son.

He helped him to not only deal with, and process the deaths of his parents, but also the fact that Bruce observed their murders first-hand. Alfred went through Bruce's growth as an adolescent into a man dealing with things like puberty, his first crush and heartbreak, and all the minute details that rearing a child brings with it. Alfred ultimately helped Bruce maneuver the path that would eventually lead him to create The Batman. Truth be told, Batman would not have gotten far without being under the watchful guidance of Mr. Pennyworth. As I consider the mythology, I understand at the center of that legend, behind the scenes and far from center stage is a benevolent man that sought not his own benefit and accolades, but to do the best he could in the upbringing of Bruce Wayne.

Another example would be Joseph, Jesus's earthly father. Joseph was a righteous dude that discovered his fiancé, Mary, was pregnant. Back then this was extremely scandalous, and to make matters worse, the child wasn't his. Mary was impregnated by God (*I'm sure that was an awkward conversation to say the least*) and sought to quietly divorce her. Nevertheless, Joseph married Mary, raised, and loved Jesus the best that he could. That is what a man with benevolence in his heart would do.

Scientist George Washington Carver once remarked, "How far you go in life depends on your being tender with the young, compassionate with the aged, sympathetic with the striving and tolerant of the weak and strong. Because someday in your life you will have been all of these."[6] Men, we should strive to help those that are unable to help themselves; this is precisely what Alfred and Joseph did. One of the most popular scriptures in the Bible is John 3:16. I'm sure most of you know it. Yet I would argue that the following verse is equally, if not more important:

"For God did not send his Son into the world to condemn the world, but to save the world through him."

John 3:17[7] NIV

God displayed His benevolence towards us in the above verse. Rather then just blasting us with judgment, He demonstrated benevolence towards us with sending Jesus into the world. We are offered a chance—a helping hand as it were—to enter into relationship with Him through His son.

**Confucius Say** Ancient Chinese philosopher Confucius was

considered to be really wise. I mean, we have been quoting him for millennia now, right? Some of my favorite nuggets of wisdom he has bestowed upon us are: Confucius say: "Man who stands on toilet, is high on pot." Confucius say: "Man who jumps off cliff, jumps to conclusion!" And don't forget, Confucius say: "A man with his hands in pockets feels foolish, but a man with holes in pockets feels nuts."[8]

In all seriousness, Confucius was a seemingly endless fount of wisdom. I find the following adage to be particularly applicable here, "To practice five things under all circumstances constitutes perfect virtue; these five are gravity, generosity of soul, sincerity, earnestness, and kindness."[9] These are powerful and timeless philosophies revolving around benevolence. The same sentiment is mirrored here:

"Stay on good terms with each other, held together by love. Be ready with a meal or a bed when it's needed. Why, some have extended hospitality to angels without ever knowing it! Regard prisoners as if you were in prison with them. Look on victims of abuse as if what happened to them had happened to you. Honor marriage, and guard the sacredness of sexual intimacy between wife and husband. God draws a firm line against casual and illicit sex."

Hebrews 13:1-4[10] MSG

We are compelled as men to look at the world in its entirety, and do what we can to improve the quality of life when and wherever we can. We have to be mindful of the macro, while focusing on our micro. Just the simple acknowledgement of a need is not good enough. The Bible proposes this:

"Suppose you see a brother or sister who has no food or clothing, and you say, "Good-bye and have a good day; stay warm and eat well"—but then you don't give that person any food or clothing. What good does that do? So you see, faith by itself isn't enough. Unless it produces good deeds, it is dead and useless."

James 2:15-17[11] NLT

Just the simple acknowledgement of a need is not good enough. It is completely worthless to see a need and not act on it if it is within your means to. Please don't confuse the awareness of someone who is in need of being treated with benevolence, with the guilt of trying to save the entire planet. There are limitations to this. When you see that a natural disaster has decimated a country or region, there is nothing on a large scale you can do. Unless that is of course, you are a man of great means. Then act. But the average Joe doesn't have that kind of pull. So what can we do? First and foremost, you can pray, and if you have some extra cash to spare, you can donate to a reputable charity or organization. What I mean more accurately is what do you have at your disposal that you can use to help others? How can you lend a hand where you're at? Mahatma Gandhi said it very well, "The simplest acts of kindness are by far more powerful then a thousand heads bowing in prayer."[12]

## Divine Instruction

The Bible is a divine instruction manual on life. It was written over a period of time spanning approximately fifteen hundred years. When you consider it in its entirety, it is a love note. The fascinating thing to me is that people look at the Bible as a rule book. A bunch of "do's" and "don'ts." I would challenge you to view it as a "how to" guide for living. A veritable "Life for Dummies" book, if you will. God is the one who has instituted and put in place these ideas. Not only is He the originator, but He is also the implementer as well. The Almighty shows his benevolence towards us in this way:

> "Or do you have no regard for the wealth of His kindness and tolerance and patience [in withholding His wrath]? Are you [actually] unaware *or* ignorant [of the fact] that God's kindness leads you to repentance [that is, to change your inner self, your old way of thinking—seek His purpose for your life]?"

> Romans 2:4[13 AMP]

Did you catch that? God's kindness leads us to repentance. Allow me to paraphrase it: God's benevolence towards us is the help we need to change our life for the good. The Almighty is benevolent to those that seek HIS help, what He desires is for us to reciprocate this, to those who need OUR help. A good boss would never ask an employee to do something that they wouldn't first do themselves. It's the same principle.

What I ask myself after I have read or heard something that impacted me is, how do I practically implement this in my life? I want to use this information in my heart, but how is it that I can apply these lessons? I know it's easier said than done. I'm quite positive we have all faced this dilemma at some point in our lives. I think it's always best to start at the most basic point, for us it is The Golden Rule.

"Do to others as you would have them do to you."

Luke 6:31 [14 NIV]

Treat people like you want to be treated. I know the multitudes proclaim this from the mountaintops, but only the devout amongst us put this into practice. An absolute talking point for most, but for us it is the point in which we both begin and end. Allow me to open it up a bit more.

"To you who are ready for the truth, I say this:
Love your enemies. Let them bring out the best in you, not the worst.
When someone gives you a hard time, respond with the energies of
prayer for that person. If someone slaps you in the face, stand there
and take it. If someone grabs your shirt, gift wrap your best coat and
make a present of it. If someone takes unfair advantage of you, use
the occasion to practice the servant life.
No more tit-for-tat stuff. Live generously.
"Here is a simple rule of thumb for behavior: Ask yourself what you
want people to do for you; then grab the initiative and do it for *them*!
If you only love the lovable, do you expect a pat on the back? Run-
of-the-mill sinners do that. If you only help those who help you, do
you expect a medal? Garden-variety sinners do that. If you only give
for what you hope to get out of it, do you think that's charity? The
stingiest of pawnbrokers does that."

This is behavior that even the most progressive amongst us tout, yet rarely walk out from day to day. It is a difficult task to be consistent in our endeavor to be benevolent. That is why this is often overlooked or even scoffed at in the locker rooms of men. Benevolence should never be viewed as a liability. But as an asset. Writer John Bunyan said, "You have not lived today until you have done something for someone who can never repay you."[16] Thus the notion of a benevolent heart of a true man is revealed to us wholly, and now we are left to ponder its mystery. However, if Jesus upped the ante with what he just said, then He went all in with what He actually did. The ultimate act of benevolence is this: sacrifice.

"Greater love hath no man than this, that a man lay down his life for his friends."
John 15:13[17] KJV

Living a sacrificial existence is the key that unlocks the door to being benevolent as men, and arguably even true happiness. It may not necessarily mean giving your life, although that could be a possibility. It may come in many different forms such as sacrificing your talents, money, or convenience. Politician William Bennett said, "A kind and compassionate act is often its own reward."[18]

A man of benevolence owns a conscience with no hubris. He doesn't always have to be right or prove his point. He doesn't need to be constantly looking out for himself. He does need to be gracious, kind, and meek. In doing this, he will ultimately become a better man. Be mindful of this warning regarding living a life lacking of benevolence:

"For judgment *will be* merciless to one who has shown no mercy; but [to the one who has shown mercy] mercy triumphs [victoriously] over judgment."

James 2:13[19] AMP

Start now, my friends. It will be too late afterwards. Once we have assumed room temperature, we will have no time to begin to choose the path of benevolence. I leave you to ponder this quote from Educator Horace Mann.

"Generosity during life is a very different thing from generosity in the hour of death; one proceeds from genuine liberality and benevolence, the other from pride or fear."[20]

# Chapter 8
## Manners And Chivalry

**manners** / *noun* / "1. ways of behaving with reference to
polite standards; social comportment:
2. a person's outward bearing; way of speaking to and
treating others:
3. characteristic or customary way of doing, making, saying,
etc.
4. air of distinction"[1]

**chivalry** / *noun* / "1. the sum of the ideal qualifications of a
knight, including courtesy, generosity, valor, and dexterity in
arms.
2. gallant warriors or gentlemen"[2]

It's been said that manners and chivalry are dead. A brief
drive through your neighborhood during traffic or a stroll
through your local grocery store should confirm this in a
rather abrupt way. It seems as if people in our society have
either completely forgotten or have never been taught
manners or the ways of chivalry. This is applicable to men in
particular, who have traditionally been the guardians of our
cultural and social mores.

This dynamic was exemplified for me by both of my parents.
As a child, my parents were relentlessly instilling proper
manners and how to conduct myself in a civilized fashion. I

was fortunate that my folks didn't want their children to be boorish, villainous little bastards (though some children weren't as lucky). Actor Fred Astaire once said, " The hardest job kids face today is learning good manners without seeing any."[3]

The very notion or idea of having to dedicate an entire chapter to this subject may be off-putting for some. I assure you it isn't. Think on this for a moment: what does it profit you to have worked so hard to move toward acquiring the qualities we have been discussing, yet remain rude or impolite? Nothing, I say! Remember, gentlemen, you can catch more bees with honey than you can with vinegar. Musician Will.i.am puts it like this, "There's no chivalry in culture any more. Sometimes you meet someone who everyone says is polite and you're like, 'Wow,' but then it's like, 'Hang on, isn't everyone supposed to be polite?"[4]

### Biblical Manners

Although the Bible isn't overtly specific about this subject, we see that Jesus was somewhat of a stickler for good manners. Look no further than the account of Simon the Pharisee and the lady with the alabaster jar. Please read the account for yourself in Luke chapter seven. However, the Cliff Note version of the story is this: Simon invited Jesus to his house for a meal. Once they arrived, a woman—who many Bible scholars believe was a prostitute—barged in and began to clean Jesus' feet with very expensive oil and her tears. She then proceeded to wipe off Jesus' feet with her hair.

Jesus was moved by this unusual gesture. The oil was estimated to be worth over a year's salary. This lady humbled herself with the demonstration of wiping His feet with her hair. It was the ultimate sign of paying Jesus honor. Making her living based upon her appearance, it stands to reason the more beautiful she was, the more money she would make. In those times, people's feet were not as, well... how could I put this? They weren't as nicely groomed as they are now. Walking around the desert and unkempt landscapes wearing nothing but flimsy Jerusalem cruisers doesn't really foster an environment for the dainty, tootsie toes we have nowadays.

All of this of course was rather offensive in the sight of the pious Pharisee. A man of Jesus' stature and reputation within the community would never had permitted such a woman to defile him in this manner. Simon questioned Jesus' quality as a teacher and man. Jesus said to him:

"Then turning toward the woman, He said to Simon, "Do you see this woman? I came into your house [but you failed to extend to Me the usual courtesies shown to a guest]; you gave Me no water for My feet, but she has wet My feet with her tears and wiped them with her hair [demonstrating her love]. You gave Me no [welcoming] kiss, but from the moment I came in, she has not ceased to kiss My feet. You did not [even] anoint My head with [ordinary] oil, but she has anointed My feet with [costly and rare] perfume."

Luke 7:44-46[5] AMP

Jesus was honored by her actions. He put Simon in his place for several things, but as it pertains to our situation: Simon's poor manners. Jesus was a guest in Simon's house, yet he had neglected to show Jesus the pleasantries that were customary to their time. The fact that Jesus called Simon out for his poor etiquette and that it has been shamefully memorialized in the Bible for all of eternity, speaks of the importance He placed on manners.

Let's take a look at a few other verses:

"God's people should be bighearted and courteous."
Titus 3:2[6] MSG

"Don't hit back; discover beauty in everyone. If you've got it in you, get along with everybody. Don't insist on getting even; that's not for you to do."

118

Romans 12:17-18[7] MSG

"Welcome people into your home and don't grumble about
it."
1 Peter 4:9[8] CEV

But the most important sentiment to convey is that of The
Golden Rule. We have gone over this in a previous chapter,
but here it is in another translation:

"Do to others whatever you would like them to do to you."
Matthew 7:12[9] NLT

There is great esteem placed upon a man's manners. I believe
that part of this quest we are on is to reestablish the qualities
that once made us so distinguished and admired throughout
history. Gentlemen, manners and chivalry most certainly are
not dead, as long as we are willing to keep them alive.
Abolitionist William Wilberforce declared, "God Almighty
has set before me two great objects: the suppression of the
slave trade and the reformation of manners."[10]

## Manners vs. Chivalry

There is a slight difference between manners and chivalry.
Not in the respect that they are in complete contrast to one
another; they are not. Nor is it that you cannot have one
without the other, they are in fact intertwined. When

approaching chivalry as men, the primary difference is that we should be compelled to be chivalrous towards women. This is not to indicate that the concept is reserved entirely for ladies only. When dealing with our fellow dudes, I would say it is more in line with decent manners, then chivalry. Politician Mike Huckabee made this correlation, "I've twice run against women opponents, and it's a very different kind of approach. For those of us who have some chivalry left, there's a level of respect... You treat some things as a special treasure; you treat other things as common."[11]

There should be something instinctual within men that compels them to want to protect and serve women. The modern feminist movement would have you to believe that this is a chauvinistic attitude or mindset. I beg to differ. As antiquated as it may seem, men have become diminished in our culture as chivalrous behavior has declined. From this moment forward, let us approach all people with manners and chivalry. Carrying on with these time-honored traditions despite the advent of technology, and contemporary norms that our culture deems acceptable. Musician Justin Timberlake noted, " That's something I learned from both my stepdad and my grandfather - that there is a thing called chivalry, and it doesn't have to die with the birth of the

Internet."[12]


## THE CHECKLISTS

Here are a few brief lists of behaviors to begin to use in your daily life. They by no means are exhaustive, nor intended to be, rather general guidelines or rules to conduct yourself with. Helpful hints for you to file in your mental iCloud for future reference and usage.


### The Madam Mandate

- Open all doors.
- Ladies first on all occasions.
- Pay for meals unless it's specifically noted otherwise.
- Walk on the outside of the sidewalk closest to the street. This keeps the lady safe and if it's rainy or snowy they will be less likely to get splashed.
- Ladies usually like being asked to dance.
- Hold the umbrella, even if you end up getting rained on.
- Offer her your jacket if she is cold.
- Pull the car up to the curb.
- Small gestures of affection go a long way.
- Always escort the lady to her front door.
- Be complimentary.
- Defend her honor, even before friends and family.
- Show interest in what she is interested in.
- LISTEN. DO NOT FIX!
- Place value and worth in her opinions.
- Be excited to meet her friends and family.
- Dear God, remember anniversaries, birthdays, and other

special occasions.

## Forkin' Manners

Table manners speak in many ways to people. You are often judged by your behavior demonstrated there. I'm no expert, so please feel free to explore this subject further. I would even recommend taking an etiquette class or two.

- Chew with your mouth closed.
- Don't talk with food in your mouth.
- Elbows off the table.
- Do not reach across someone seated at the table, politely ask them to hand you whatever you may need.
- Wait until everyone is served before you eat.
- Refrain from shoving entire pieces of food in your mouth that are bigger than bite. (*That's why God created knives*).
- Always use a napkin to wipe your mouth.
- When napkin is not in use, it should be placed on your lap.
- Your utensils are not drumsticks.
- If you are full, stop eating!
- If you do not care for what was served, try to eat a little bit of it, or at least cut it up and make it look like you tried to.
- If you have to spit something out, do it discretely into your napkin.
- If you have to leave the table prematurely, excuse yourself.
- If a lady must excuse herself, it is customary for gentlemen to stand.
- Keep all electronic devices off the table while eating.
- If you are out with people, turn your phone on vibrate.

- Unless it is an absolute emergency, don't respond to that text. Whoever it is can wait.

## Technological Manners

Don't allow technology to rob you of your manners.

- Don't text while you are in the middle of a conversation with someone.
- Reply to emails within 24 to 48 hours.
- Keep voicemails brief and to the point, leaving only pertinent and contact information.
- Emotional infliction is undetectable in text form. Remember that while both sending and receiving written communications (texts and emails).

## Road Rage

Vehicular aggression has gotten the best of us all. Don't let it get you down. Read up and apply.

- Wave as a gesture of thanks when someone lets you over in traffic.
- Offer an apology when you make a careless maneuver in front of someone.
- Don't be afraid to use your blinkers.
- Scoot up as far as you can when making a left turn. The people behind you may need to turn right or pass you.
- It's ok to allow people in your lane in traffic (*You're not at the Daytona 500*).

- The right lane is for cruising; the left is for accelerating.
- When stopped by the police, pull over and out of the way as to not block traffic.
- When pulled over by the police, be polite, refer to them as officer, and obey them.
- Don't text and drive.
- DON'T DRINK AND DRIVE!
- If you're sleepy, pull over as soon as you can and take a catnap, or listen to comedy. It is impossible to sleep while you are laughing.

## Party-quette

While attending social gatherings, this is how to conduct yourself.

- When you get an invite, RSVP as soon as you know you can attend.
- Don't RSVP and then not show unless a valid reason is offered.
- If you're invited to a party, ask the host what you can bring.
- Not sure what to bring? Snacks, sweets, or beverages are always appreciated.
- Help clean up after a party. Even if no one else does.
- Always send a note of thanks (*or at the very least, call or text*).
- Never show up with an unannounced guest. Ask the host if you can brin someone not on the guest list, and let them know who it is you wish to bring.
- Always say good-bye to the hosts.

# Common Decency

These are considered applicable for most all occasions.
Please feel free to use generously.

- Proper hygiene is always appropriate (*and appreciated!*)
- Stand, if possible, for the playing of the National Anthem.
- Stand, if possible, and place your right hand over your heart when reciting The Pledge of Allegiance.
- Say "Please," "Thank You," and "You're Welcome." And say them often.
- When you drop someone off, wait until they get inside to pull away.
- Refer to people as "Ma'am" and "Sir."
- Offer a hardy handshake when you meet someone. Your handshake says a lot about who you are as a man.
- Always use "Hello" and "Goodbye."
- Apologize when you accidentally bump into someone.
- Be on time. Being constantly late, shows you have little respect for others.
- Be polite and courteous. Even if they don't deserve it.
- Put the toilet seat down *(Ladies you're welcome)*.
- If you miss a meeting, apologize and ask to reschedule.
- Don't allow your children to be the physical embodiment of a tornado at someone else's house. If they are, for the love of everything Holy, clean, fix or replace damaged items.
- Remove your hat in sacred or professional places.
- Your attire and behavior should coincide with the environment you are in.
- Check in with your loved ones. Just let them know you arrived safely and when they can expect you home.
- When you get up to grab something for yourself, ask others if they want anything while you are up.
- Be kind to those working in the service, retail, or medical

professions who are taking care of you.

- Don't be a tightwad, tip well. Especially if they deserve it.
- It is alright to say Merry Christmas, Happy Easter, Happy Thanksgiving, Happy Passover, Happy Hanukkah, Happy Festivus or whatever seasonal greeting is appropriate during the particular time of the year.
- If someone offers a seasonal greeting to you, and you are not affiliated with that particular holiday, don't take it offensively. How are they to know? They are simply extending a polite salutation to you.
- Respect yourself. It will be a lot easier to respect others if you do.

Do not be overwhelmed by these lists. It takes practice, and patience, along with stick-to-it-iv-ness to develop these behavioral traits. It is important to keep this in mind: someone else's bad manners are no excuse for you to negate good manners. Author H. Jackson Browne, Jr. put it like this, "Good manners sometimes means simply putting up with other people's bad manners."[13] You may be a stalwart and debonair man, yet if you're intrusive and discourteous it matters none whatsoever.

In my experience, how you conduct yourself is just as important as what, or who you know.

Keep this in mind: those who have good manners and

chivalry, yet have minor flaws will always be preferred over perceived perfection accompanied by rudeness. Why? Because skills can be taught, honed, and acquired far more easily then manners can be instilled to those who lack such qualities. Supreme Court Justice Clarence Thomas said, "Good manners will open doors that the best education cannot."[14]

I think the following says it best:

"Manners Maketh Man"[15]
– Headmaster Wiliam Horman

"Be polite, be professional, but have a plan to kill everybody you meet."[16]
– General James "Mad Dog" Mattis

# Chapter 9
## A Warrior's Mentality

**warrior** / *noun* / "1. a person engaged or experienced in warfare; soldier.
a person who shows or has shown great vigor, courage, or aggressiveness, as in politics or athletics."[1]

**mentality** / *noun* / "1. capacity or endowment:
2. the set of one's mind; view; outlook"[2]

This is the one chapter that I believe is distinctly different from the others. Primarily due to the fact that what we have already discussed are basic tenants of moral decency that are not necessarily gender-specific. Our genetic makeup gives us a difference in approach and attitude towards the various topics of discussion, but all of human kind can benefit from what we have shared.

What I mean more precisely is that at our core, at our very essence, every one of us men have something that is primal, brutal, and if it is not properly tempered, can become uncontrollable.

Hidden within the deep, dark crevices of a man's heart, lies the capacity for barbarism and savagery. We may not want to admit it. Society may tell us to suppress it. We may have tried our best to avoid it, but they are there. Gaze into a mirror, my friend. Look yourself right in the eyes. Do a gut check. Tell me I'm wrong. I know it is scary to acknowledge and behold, yet acknowledge and behold we must.

This is one of the most critical components we men bear. Most of us have been taught, and our culture has been passive-aggressively nuancing us to death, that we should resist these instinctual urges. The overwhelming and subversive measures that have been taken to undermine the warrior inside all of us men is nothing short of astonishing. However, now is time for the dormant fighter in us to arise. Do you see your adversary taking position on the horizon? The drums of war are beating strong and defiantly ever so faintly in the distance. Can you hear them? Do you feel the pounding of their synchronized march advancing towards you? Good. Embrace it. Run to the battle head high, chest out, screaming boldly like the valiant warrior you are!

However, if this does not resonate inside of you, read on my friend. Read on and together we will awaken the warrior within.

Let me make one thing clear, and this is vitally important. Just because the propensity to commit violence is in your heart, that doesn't make you a warrior—let alone a man. A warrior has the mentality that he will only fight for what is necessary. He defends what is pure, and true and does so in a noble way. Displaying behavior in any other capacity is diametrically opposed to what we will be highlighting here, actually it makes you a coward. In preparing for this chapter, I thought a lot about the film *Braveheart*. Mel Gibson does a fantastic job of encapsulating the mentality of a warrior. The following dialogue should help illustrate my point. As his father Malcom is headed off to war, young William Wallace looks at him and says, "I can fight." Malcom answers, "I know. I know you can fight. But it's our wits that make us men."[3]

"There are three types of people in this world: sheep, wolves, and sheepdogs. Some people prefer to believe that evil doesn't exist in the world, and if it ever darkened their doorstep, they wouldn't know how to protect themselves. Those are the sheep. Then you've got predators who use violence to prey on the weak. They're the wolves. And then there are those blessed with the gift of aggression, an overpowering need to protect the flock. These men are the rare breed who live to confront the wolf. They are the sheepdog."[4] This quote from the film *American Sniper* is perfect for what we will be discussing throughout this chapter. In part, this is what defines us as men, and allows us to have a warrior's mentality.

### Spiritual Warriors

If you're a pacifist, I imagine this might be rubbing you the wrong way. I can see how this topic may go against the grain for some. Please don't think for a moment that I dismiss those feelings. Do not feel discounted as a man either. How about you and I conduct and experiment? Alright, let's think about the man, Jesus. Picture Him as you have before in the past. Now picture Him in the stories that you may have been told as a child. Picture him in the fields with the little sheep. If the Jesus you pictured looks like Barry Gibb from The Bee Gees wearing a robe, sandals, and sporting a great tan, stop right there.

Jesus was no tree-hugging hippie wearing long robes with gorgeous flowing hair, and a smooth, flawless complexion. He didn't smell like patchouli oil or sing kumbaya. Jesus was the ultimate warrior. You disagree? OK. Let us examine the evidence. Jesus was a carpenter by trade. Most carpenters I know are fairly tough dudes, right? In His day, there were no hardware or lumber stores. We're talking about a guy who had to go find the wood himself, then cut it down. With No chainsaw or any other tools of convenience that we take for granted. He then had to bring it back to his workspace. Whittle it down to a manageable size, and turn it into whatever he was commissioned to create. So for practical reasons alone, Jesus was jacked.

Also, consider that Jesus was beaten and spat on. He was flogged thirty-nine times, one short of a death sentence. The whip had nine leather lashes, with metal balls at he end of each tail, and often had shards of bone laced throughout. Chunks of flesh were torn from his body, and most experts agree that his spine was nearly exposed. He then had a crown of thorns put on his head, and a robe was placed on his back only to be ripped off once His wounds began to scab. And if that wasn't bad enough, He then proceeded to carry a cross—which was the ultimate instrument of His demise—up a hill. Once on top of the hill, He had nails driven through His wrists and ankles. As He hung, He was slowly asphyxiated and eventually His heart had burst.

Let me assure you that Jesus was no meager flower child off on some delusional euphoric hippy-dippy love trip. He was a warrior sent on a mission that he had to complete. And while He is God, He is more of a man than you or I will ever be.

In the book of Matthew, Jesus once got ticked off when travelers coming from long distances to sacrifice at the temple were taken advantage of. Merchants that sold these people what they needed to fulfill their religious obligations, as well as the moneychangers that were exchanging their foreign currency were exploiting them. Jesus saw this and it filled Him with righteous indignation. Here is the account found in Matthew:

"And Jesus entered the temple [grounds] and drove out [with force] all who were buying and selling [birds and animals for sacrifice] in the temple *area*, and He turned over the tables of the moneychangers [who made a profit exchanging foreign money for temple coinage] and the chairs of those who were selling doves [for sacrifice]. Jesus said to them, "It is written [in Scripture], 'My house shall be called a house of prayer'; but you are making it a robbers' den."

Matthew 21:12-13[5] AMP

Jesus hates injustice and seeing people mistreated and taken advantage of. When you read this account in John chapter two, it actually said that Jesus had fashioned a whip to drive these scoundrels out of the temple. You see Jesus was fully aware that there would come times in a man's life when we would have to stand up and fight. Jesus didn't shy away from this, or try to present it in a big shiny bow. He instructed us, as men, to contend with these troubles when they came calling, not cower in fear or intimation. Jesus told us:

"From the days of John the Baptist until now the kingdom of heaven suffers violent assault, and violent men seize it by force [as a precious prize]."

Matthew 11:12[5] AMP

Despite the fact that many people think that "Hippy Jesus" was a peacenik, He wasn't. He knew intimately of the wars, both seen and unseen, that would need to be waged. As a matter of fact, He bestowed a special blessing upon these warriors:

"Blessed are the peacemakers, for they will be called children of
God."
Matthew 5:9[6] NIV

He called these blessed peacemakers His children. We must acknowledge the fact that there is a vast difference between a "peacemaker" and a "peacekeeper." Peacekeepers attempt to defuse situations before they begin, no matter the long-term effect. It is strategic calculation with only a short-term objective in sight. No goals of genuine long-lasting peace. There is an argument that could be made for one such person rationalizing that they are putting wisdom into practice, and I can see that. However, there is a time for every purpose under Heaven and upon Earth. There is a time to try to MAINTAIN peace, and then there are times when you have to MAKE peace. The problems come when all you are doing is continually putting out these fires. The embers are still smoldering and it takes very little for the sparks to fly. There is no resolution, so the ill feelings linger on. The peacemakers see the conflict and resolve it. They squash it. Whether by diplomatic means or not, the end result is true peace. That is not always easy, nor is it comfortable. Most people are scared to death of confrontation, and that right there is the problem.

We deceive ourselves by thinking if we are just nice enough, loving enough, or tolerant enough, that times of trouble will pass over us. This is seldom the case. Historically, for certain, but if you evaluate the course of your own life you may begin to understand and see a pattern developing. I know that when I have tried to deal with long-term conflicts passively, rarely does it ever get permanently resolved. It isn't until I have said "enough's enough" and took a stand, did the tensions end.

I laugh to myself when I hear people that follow the teachings of Jesus talk about how He was a peaceful man and that as His disciples we must follow suit. I laugh because I fear that they don't have a firm grasp of what He actually taught. I agree He was a loving and peaceful man and that we must follow His example, in which case Jesus Himself said the following:

> "Do not suppose that I have come to bring peace to the earth.
> I did not come to bring peace, but a sword."
> Matthew 10:34[6] NIV

Jesus knew that we would encounter troubles while living on earth. He wanted us to be aware that we would have times when there would be no peace to be found, and in fact, there would be wars and conflicts that we will be engaged in. Oftentimes our own families will be the ones who we battle with the most fiercely, and frequently. The only consistent source of peace any of us will find is in Him. He not only wanted to open our eyes to this fact, but to be prepared also:

"He said to them, "But now let the one who has a moneybag take it, and likewise a knapsack. And let the one who has no sword sell his cloak and buy one.""

Luke 22:36[7] ESV

Gentlemen, Jesus told us to get a sword! A sword isn't one of those handy dandy multi-tools with a screwdriver, bottle opener, compass, saw, knife, spork, or whatever else they can cram into it. A sword has one solitary purpose. It is a weapon, plain and simple. It is used for fighting. The only duality it may have is solely dependent upon the wielder of said weapon, whether its function is intended for defensive or offensive use. Jesus was saying acquire whatever items and skills necessary for when those moments come and you must fight.

As we read these verses, did it cause you to pause and think? Did it challenge you and what you had previously perceived? Good. That was the purpose. We need to begin to understand what it means to not only carry with us a warrior's mentality, but we must comprehend what that genuinely means. When, where, and (more importantly) how, to become that man.

Remember this: essentially Jesus came down to earth to pick a fight with the devil. He saw the tyranny afflicted on those of us who live in the flesh by those who inhabit the spirit. He wanted us to be free and He knew that would mean He would have to fight for us. Jesus beat the devil with a big wooden stick for you and I. It was not fought in a boastful or arrogant manner. Nor was this war waged out of wrong motives and hasty actions. It was bloody, painful, and ultimately lead Jesus to give His life to win the war.

### Bullying, Bothering, & Other Instruments of Torture

The national spotlight has been focused on bullying now more then ever. There are even different categories of bullying. Of course, there's the time-honored traditional physical and verbal bullying, but with the advent of social media, we now have cyber bullying too. I don't pretend to know what it's like to be a young person dealing with this kind of torment. After school, whatever extracurricular activities I was involved with had finished, I could escape by going home or hanging out with my friends. I was able to find a solace that modern technology does not forward people today. My heart does sincerely go out to these victims.

Even so, we know that there is nothing new under the sun. What issues we now face are a result of the human condition, which is perpetually unchanging. I was bullied. My friends were bullied. My dad and his dad were bullied, and so on and so forth. If bullying has been around for thousands of years, why is it being so focused on right now? Why is there currently so much anti-bullying rhetoric? Where was the outcry from previous generations? What has changed and why? Could it be us? Could it be that men have become sissified in our culture?

As I look back on my life, I can honestly say I am glad I was bullied. It educated and challenged me in ways that I may not have been otherwise. I learned to establish boundaries and that I don't have to take people's garbage. I learned to stand up for others and myself. It helped me sharpen and develop a keen sense of observing people's motives and intentions. It's what Martial Artist Bruce Lee referred to as, "The Art of fighting without fighting."[8] More importantly, it helped me develop a thick skin. This is an attribute that has helped me tremendously through my life.

What being bullied effectively taught me was how to respond rather than to react. Big difference, fellas. Reacting is unchecked instincts. Responding is a calculated maneuver. Responding requires discipline, reacting does not. If you can solve a problem diplomatically, then by all means, do so. Violence should never be your first reaction. However, if you can learn to respond, you maybe able to defend yourself and avoid any unnecessary physical escalation.

Actor Chuck Norris has said, "Violence is my last option."[9] When I was growing up, my dad would never push me to fight. That was never the direction that he would point me towards. What he did say to me was, "You better never start a fight, but if you do get into one, you had better be the one to finish it." I remember like it was yesterday—him showing me how to Box. I can still hear him saying, "Put your hands up. Guard your face. Okay, now slip the jab, slip the jab." It works like this: if you go looking for trouble, chances are you will find it. But if trouble knocks on your doorstep, you don't have to invite it in for tea and crumpets either. I'm going to shoot straight with you; we have to learn to stand up to bullies.

I think the issue is that we are conditioned to believe that we do not have the ability, or the right, to stand up for ourselves. That we must endure the torment until we reach that point in our lives where we stop having to deal with it. But that is a fallacy. Not only does it not let up, but the older you get, the more intensified it becomes.

What concerns me is the lack of preparation for life that cowering down to adversarial situations causes. When I was bullied, or saw other's bullied, and stood up to it, it was essentially a lesson in how to prepare myself for manhood. I fear that we may be coddling too much, thus creating generations of victims unequipped to handle the battles that life will throw their way. Need I remind you that life is a battle for which there is no retreat, no safe zone, or panic room we can permanently hold ourselves up in to escape the harsh realities and uncomfortable circumstances we will encounter.

You don't have to be an expert in hand-to-hand combat in order to do what is good when it comes to defending what you believe in. You just need to have a sense of right and wrong and a willingness to protect that which is true. Here is the sacred charge we have been given:

> "You're here to defend the defenseless, to make sure that underdogs get a fair break;
> Your job is to stand up for the powerless, and prosecute all those who exploit them."
>
> Psalm 82:4[10] MSG

Do not fret if you ever think you are inadequate or incapable of such things. We have all discounted ourselves at times; it is only natural. Trust me when I tell you that you are in good company. General George S. Patton once said, "If we take the generally accepted definition of bravery as a quality which knows no fear, I have never seen a brave man. All men are frightened. The more intelligent they are, the more they are frightened."[11] Patton also said, "Courage is fear holding on a minute longer."[11] God is amazing. He doesn't call the equipped; He equips the called. We see through the course of human history ordinary men, like you and I, being able to accomplish extraordinary feats of courage and bravery with the divine hand of Providence at our six.

When it comes to the subject of bullying, we can, and must do better raising our children to be the kind of people who stand against bullies, not become one.

Be an example. Demonstrate virtuous character. Show them the way.

## The Way of the Warrior

Author Carlos Castaneda commented, "To be a warrior is not a simple matter of wishing to be one. It is rather an endless struggle that will go on to the very last moment of our lives. Nobody is born a warrior, in exactly the same way that nobody is born an average man. We make ourselves into one or the other."[12] Do you remember when I mentioned that responding requires discipline, reacting does not? This is the way of the warrior.

Discipline, or to be more specific self-discipline, is what separates a warrior from the average run of the mill couch potato. This separates because it isn't easy. If it were, everyone would be self-disciplined. It demands a man be consistent in developing and maintaining routines that ships him into shape. And I don't just mean physical fitness. President Harry S. Truman said, "In reading the lives of great men, I found that the first victory they won was over themselves... self-discipline with all of them came first."[13]

Responding, much like self-discipline requires practice. It demands to be evaluated again and again. It is well-rehearsed; like muscle memory, if you will. Reacting is impulsive and compulsive. There's nothing rehearsed, and no muscle has been developed to save memories to. It does not possess wisdom, but in fact is irreverent and lacks self-control. It takes time to commit to becoming self-disciplined in any art form. While leaning to conquer one's urges, they customarily will do all that they can to resist self-discipline, these are often more of an adversary then any other physical opponent or problem could ever be. We have been given the ability to defeat our shortcomings, and even our own laziness when we apply these principles and become disciplined.

"For God did not give us a spirit of timidity *or* cowardice *or* fear, but [He has given us a spirit] of power and of love and of sound judgment *and* personal discipline [abilities that result in a calm, well-balanced mind and self-control]."

2 Timothy 1:7[14] AMP

As we dissect this verse, we discover that The Almighty hasn't put fear into our hearts. He hasn't designed us to embrace timidity or cowardice. He has created us to be powerful; and has endowed us with the capacity to love. More importantly, we see that God has given us the ability to be self-disciplined. We can look at this and understand that it is self-discipline that enables us to operate in the spirit of power and of love and of good judgment.

The Apostle Paul discusses discipline and compares it to being an athlete:

> "Do you not know that in a race all the runners run [their very best to win], but only one receives the prize? Run [your race] in such a way that you may seize the prize *and* make it yours! Now every athlete who [goes into training and] competes in the games is disciplined *and* exercises self-control in all things. They do it to win a crown that withers, but we [do it to receive] an imperishable [crown that cannot wither]. Therefore I do not run without a definite goal; I do not flail around like one beating the air [just shadow boxing]. But [like a boxer] I strictly discipline my body and make it my slave"
>
> 1 Corinthians 9:24-27a[15] AMP

I like these verses for several reasons. First and foremost, Paul talks about runners and the discipline required of them to compete competitively. This is because life is not a sprint; it's a marathon. Although to do well in either, training and discipline most definitely are required. The discipline it takes to train and run a marathon is entirely different from a sprint. Marathons are lengthy, and they take a longer time to finish. It isn't the brief dash, which one thinks of with sprinting. I have friends who run marathons that are over one hundred miles long. The stamina and endurance it takes to perform at that level is incredible. You have to be self-disciplined to devote yourself to mastering it.

The second reason I like Paul's analogy is because he refers to boxing, basically fighting. Paul is saying that he disciplines himself to be a warrior. The wars we will wage will call for tactful accuracy and intelligence. Men we cannot be intimidated nor cower down to fear. When the moment comes and we have to fight, we must do so in the spirit of power, love, and wisdom after committing to the riggers of discipline. Discipline is a little thing that will make a big difference in your effectiveness as a warrior, and a man.

I want to draw your attention to something you may have possibly overlooked: self-discipline. Contemplate that for a moment. It is called SELF-discipline because YOU yourself have to determine to be disciplined. No one else can make that decision for you. And no one else can traverse through the systematic undertaking to be disciplined that you will embark on. It's entirely up to you.
We were neither born to be a warrior nor to be average. It is our

choice. You as a man have the ultimate say in what you will become. Know that you have the ability to start right now to become disciplined. You can create a routine of self-discipline in twenty one days. Three brief weeks is all that is needed to change your life forever. 504 hours to begin to carry out the training physically, mentally, spiritually, and emotionally to become a better man. Leadership expert John C. Maxwell has said, "Most people want to avoid pain, and discipline is usually painful."[16]

It is incumbent upon us to stand against evil. Statesman Edmund Burke spoke this simple truth so poignantly, "The only thing necessary for the triumph of evil is for good men to do nothing."[17] That which destroys evil is good. Good lays siege to the power of evil, and arises victoriously. This is what compels us to cheer for our heroes. We all root for the good guys, and wait with bated breath for the defeat of the evil foe. I believe it's in that same spirit that prompted President Ronald Reagan to say, There is no choice between peace and war. Only fight or surrender."[18] The scriptures say this about doing good in the face of evil:

"Who is going to harm you if you are eager to do good? But even if you should suffer for what is right, you are blessed. "Do not fear their threats; do not be frightened."

1 Peter 3:13-14[19] NIV

It isn't always easy to acknowledge the moments in our own lives when we are the ones being tormented. Sometimes, it's easier to see wrongs being done to others while the silent wars we wage in our own hearts and minds go unnoticed. In saying all of this, we must be aware of those around us who suffer, yet not be so preoccupied we cannot see when it is the fortress of our own soul that is under assault. If your enemy can keep you occupied and stunted, you will not be able to help others in their time of need, thus rendering you completely ineffective as a warrior.

## The BraveHearted

Fear not, gentlemen. YOU ARE A WARRIOR. A hard-fought victory is within your grasp. We return to the wisdom of General Patton who said, "Wars may be fought with weapons, but they are won by men."[20] People may laugh and scoff, and of course your opponent will not fall easily. But when you know what is worth defending, you do so at all costs. This piece of dialogue from *Captain America: Civil War,* is inspirational and befitting to this chapter, "Compromise where you can. Where you can't, don't. Even if everyone is telling you that something wrong is something right. Even if the whole world is telling you to move, it is your duty to plant yourself like a tree, look them in the eye, and say, 'No, you move'."[21]

We are all in this fight together. The high tide makes all ships rise, so it is when men come together. We will either stand as brothers in arms, or we fall separately. We help each other fight and take our stance regardless of position or status. Do not think for a second that one man is more capable or better equipped than another. That is rubbish. I have my shortcomings, and you have yours. When a brother tastes the bitterness of defeat, we must come to his aid, help heal his wounds, and get him back on that field of battle. No man is an island. It is the precise point that Pastor Martin Niemöller was trying to drive home in his poem "First They Came…"

"First they came for the Socialists, and I did not speak out—
Because I was not a Socialist.
Then they came for the Trade Unionists, and I did not speak out—
Because I was not a Trade Unionist.
Then they came for the Jews, and I did not speak out—
Because I was not a Jew.
Then they came for me—and there was no one left to speak for me."[22]

My fellow sheepdogs, I admonish you in the sight of The Almighty to embrace a Warrior's Mentality and advance. Advance forward and fight, I say! For the hour of history in which we find ourselves occupying is calling, and demanding that men emerge. There is too much at stake for you to be out of the game. Too many battles in the war of life that need to be fought and won. Too many awaiting the freedom and deliverance that only you can contend for. You will fight those fears and win. You will look those bullies in the eye and say "No More!" You will no longer allow those ghosts that haunt get the best of you. You will stop the wolves from stalking the sheep. You will be a peacemaker and no longer a peacekeeper. Rise up, beat your chest, and unleash the howl that has been lying dormant in your heart and soul. The time has come. You were put here to chew bubble gum and kick ass, and, fellas, there ain't no more bubble gum to be chewed.

Contemplate President Reagan's words, "Peace is not absence of conflict, it is the ability to handle conflict by peaceful means."[23] Warriors have witnessed first hand the carnage of the innocent, and they would seek alternative, more amicable methods to achieve their objectives. Therefore, they will seek diplomatic means for resolution and forgo a conflict if at all possible. A warrior knows the difference between a legitimate battle to fight, and one that would yield fruitless results. Some wars are just not ours to wage. A warrior will not fight for personal gain, or wealth. That's what mercenaries fight for. Nevertheless, once a warrior has suited up for battle and has committed in his heart to fight, watch out!

Men, none of us are guaranteed one more breath. Now is the time, my fellow warriors, this is the hour we stand, take up arms, and ride into war, together.

"You have come to fight as free men, and free men you are. What will you do with that freedom? Will you fight? Aye, fight and you may die. Run, and you'll live... at least a while. And dying in your beds, many years from now, would you be willin' to trade ALL the days, from this day to that, for one chance, just one chance, to come back here and tell our enemies that they may take our lives, but they'll never take... OUR FREEDOM!"[24]

# Chapter 10
## Humility

**humility** / *noun* / "the quality or condition of being humble; modest opinion or estimate of one's own importance, rank, etc"[1]

I understand it may sound pretentious to speak about humility. We think the worst thing in the world is to eat a big slice of humble pie. Trust me, I know, and it isn't. There are many different variations of humble pie, but the one common denominator that runs through them all is that each one tastes bittersweet. The bitter reminds us to avoid repeating the same mistakes. The sweet comes in hindsight, which is always 20/20. As we grow from our experiences and become humbled by them, we have the sweetness of knowing we can avoid the potential bitter pain and pitfalls from experiences of our past.

Having to eat humble pie is never something we want to do. Yet we have the opportunity to display our quality when we are able to swallow each and every last morsel. I love how Actor George Clooney talks about this, "I watch 'Batman & Robin' from time to time. It's the worst movie I ever made, so it's a good lesson in humility."[2]

Humility is extremely important to learn, particularly for men. Often, after men have great, long-fought victories, we tend to begin to develop a Big Head. That is to be expected to some degree. However, there is a huge difference between a brief celebratory boast and walking around perpetually conceited. We talked about this in chapter seven when we addressed benevolence. Benevolence goes hand in hand with humility. Not that they are the same thing, but they share similar attributes. The aptitude needed to be benevolent is nearly identical to that of humility.

## Proudly Humble

There are references in nearly every culture pertaining to virtues and vices that one should embrace and resist. You may call them "the seven deadly sins." The scriptures do not refer to them as such, however it does mention a list of six things God hates and one He loathes:

"These six things the Lord hates; Indeed, seven are repulsive to Him:
A proud look [the attitude that makes one overestimate oneself and discount others],
a lying tongue,
And hands that shed innocent blood,
A heart that creates wicked plans,
Feet that run swiftly to evil,
A false witness who breathes out lies [even half-truths],
And one who spreads discord (rumors) among brothers."

Proverbs 6:16-19[3] AMP

Pride perpetually battles against humility. These forces will always be at odds with one another. But it is simply a matter of recognizing them, and not allowing prides foot in the door. The Almighty opposes pride, as we read above. Pride is the Pandora's Box that, once opened, allows other things to be unleashed in your life. However, God gives us the assistance we need:

"Though He scoffs at the scoffers *and* scorns the scorners,
Yet He gives His grace [His undeserved favor] to the humble [those who give up self-importance]."

Proverbs 3:34[3] AMP

As we stumble towards living in a genuine state of humility, we must ask for help. The traditional thought is that as men we can make it on our own. We'll figure it out. We say to others, "I got this," right? No, not right. One of the first steps to embracing humility is being humble enough to recognize that we do need assistance. God extends grace and mercy, though we have not earned it, nor deserve it—all that is needed is to simply ask.

Actor Michael J. Fox once said, "Humility is always a good thing. It's always a good thing to be humbled by circumstances so you can then come from a sincere place to try to deal with them."[4] This is the objective that we should have when we gaze upon our life. These circumstances that we go through are the very items hidden in the toolbox of the Almighty to straighten out our life. Look at it like this: The master mechanic will be using the wrench of humility to tighten and loosen up the different nuts and bolts of our engine to achieve our optimal performance.

Humility is one of the best tools to gauge our perception of everything in life. If we think too highly of ourselves, we believe we are invincible. That we can literally walk through walls, and have bullets bounce off of our chest. We even begin to think that all of our decisions and reactions to people are always correct. We rarely take the time to consider the consequences of our actions, how they affect us and, most importantly, how they impact others. Aerosmith Frontman Steven Tyler said, "Humility is really important because it keeps you fresh and new."[5]

At twenty-six, I believed I was impenetrable. I had a game plan for my live and was beginning to execute said plan. Marriage, house, kids, career, etc. One average September morning, I woke up and saw something floating around in my left eye. An appointment to the eye doctor was made for my next day off, and that was all I thought of it. At the appointment, my doctor took just one look at my eyes, and I could tell by his reaction alone it wasn't good. He forcefully pulled me out of the examination room into his office and slammed the door! Needless to say, I was getting really concerned. He asked some questions about my health history, and my family's background. He told me that in the thirty plus years practicing ophthalmology he had never seen anyone whose eyes were as bad as mine. He said what I saw floating around was blood. It looked to him as if my eyes had been hemorrhaging for several decades. As you can imagine, that wasn't the news I was expecting to hear. He immediately sent me to see a retina specialist.

Still not fully appreciating the magnitude of the crap storm I was in, I thought this was no big deal. Surely with all of the medical breakthroughs you hear about, something can be done. No sweat. He went through all of the tests at his disposal, and then some. At the end of the day I was patiently waiting to hear the results. His assistant called me back from the waiting room to his office. While in his office, he spouted out all of the medical jargon one may expect. Having no idea as to what he was specifically saying I just asked him point blank, "Doc, are you telling me I COULD go blind?" He said, "No. I am telling you that you ARE going blind." I felt like I was hit by a ton of bricks. It was one of those surreal moments you see in the movies where the world is still spinning around really fast but the character sees everything in slow motion.

When I finally came to, I heard my family sobbing. I was beginning to understand the gravity of the situation. Over the course of time I had over two-dozen laser surgeries to cauterize the hemorrhaging in my eyes. The scar tissue that developed as a result from all of the laser operations eventually attached to my retinas causing them to become detached. I had three vitrectomy procedures, a cataract removed (*and a partridge in a pear tree*). The end result is that I am legally blind. I have limited vision in one eye, and none in the other. I am not able to drive, and I need special devices to help me navigate through life.

I share this because I was handed a much-needed dose of humility. The fact is that before all of this I was headstrong, and thought way too highly of myself. I was an arrogant mannish boy. I needed cast down from my lofty position. And for that, I am grateful. This changed my approach to everything in life. I began to empathize with others and the world that surrounded me. I started feeling a new emotion called compassion.

My point being is that even though the process I went through was not what I would have chosen, it is the path that I was assigned. As I continue to go through this, as well as other issues in my life, I am getting even closer to being the person my dog thinks I am. I'm convinced that one of the reasons I went through this was because there is a world outside of myself that, although I knew existed in theory, I was ignorant of in a practical manner. Ironically, I was having trouble with my vision, but suddenly I became able to see the needs and afflictions of those that I walked by everyday, and for the first time cared and attempted to help. This was something that while seated high upon my thrown of pride I was unable, nor did I care, to see. The scriptures says:

"Therefore humble yourselves under the mighty hand of God [set aside self-righteous pride], so that He may exalt you [to a place of honor in His service] at the appropriate time"

1 Peter 5:6[6] AMP

Quarterback Tim Tebow put it like this, "So much of how we act and what we do is based on humility or pride - that's everything. And when you can humble yourself, you know, we are more like Christ when we can humble ourselves."[7] Tebow went on to say, "We have to humble ourselves and the way you do that is by serving other people."[7] It is through humility that we can serve others, which is what we discussed in chapter seven with benevolence. Servanthood is sincerely one of life's most sacred callings, and one we should all aspire to. For it is within servanthood that we fulfill the longings of our heart, and become who we are destined to be as a man.

# The Destructive Power of Yes

Pride is something that we rarely notice in ourselves, which is why we are often the last to see when we have been walking in it. This is the precise reason we need to have people around us who will love us enough to punch us in the stones when we start behaving arrogantly. Many have fallen prey to the nature of pride. Since we understand that humility is a righteous virtue, pride therefore is an unrighteous vice. The sin of pride was what ultimately caused Lucifer to fall *(check out Ezekiel 28 and Isaiah 14 for further explanation)*. So in response we must know that the devil is also trying to make us fall victim to pride. The Bible says this:

> Be sober [well balanced and self-disciplined], be alert *and* cautious at all times. That enemy of yours, the devil, prowls around like a roaring lion [fiercely hungry], seeking someone to devour.

> 1 Peter 5:8[6 AMP]

Having people around us who will say the hard things, like *no*, and point out when we slip into the foggy mist of pride is of the utmost importance. For if we are not able to detect when we are in this danger zone, we must have people around us that will blast the siren of truth to warn us from drifting too far from humility's shore.

Yet so often we surround ourselves with people who tell us what they think we WANT to hear, not what we NEED to hear. In my estimation, this is just basic human nature; no one enjoys being the barer of bad news. Perhaps they don't want to hurt your feelings, or maybe they are afraid of how you will react to them. Regardless, this is not helpful at all. The scriptures reveal this truth:

"Faithful are the wounds of a friend [who corrects out of love and concern],
But the kisses of an enemy are deceitful [because they serve his hidden agenda]."

Proverbs 27:6[8] AMP

It's imperative you fill your life with people who love you enough to tell you the truth. Surrounding yourself with "Yes Men" will not benefit you whatsoever. People who tell you what you want to hear only escort you closer to the brink of destruction. If your support system is not helping you be responsible during moments of success, as well as failure, they aren't fulfilling their duties. As NBA Superstar LeBron James puts it, "You know, my family and friends have never been yes-men: 'Yes, you're doing the right thing, you're always right.' No, they tell me when I'm wrong, and that's why I've been able to stay who I am and stay humble."[9]

We need to cherish the ones we have in our lives who will tell us the hard things, the things we don't want to hear. The ones that shove a deep, dark, and truthful mirror in our face and make us stare at what we are and what we are possibly becoming. That is true love.

It isn't always life circumstances that help keep us humble. It is the daring ones that love us recklessly enough to risk hurting our feelings in order for us to become better men. The one thing I have discovered is that this is a two way street. Just as you are reliant upon their perspective in your life, they become reliant and permissive of your help also.

Another important facet to having people in our life that help us navigate the terrain of humility is not as obvious. There is a difference between humility, and believing you are worthless. Worthlessness is thinly veiled in a garment that, when worn, and presented in a certain slant of light, looks an awful lot like humility. Worthlessness, like pride, is easy to misjudge. But make no mistake about it, worthlessness is an even more destructive ruse than pride.

When we embrace worthlessness, we become paralyzed with an infirmity that is nearly impossible to cure on our own. When we feel worthless we tear ourselves down, and that is the difference. Worthlessness makes us walk around with our head and eyes cast down low. Humility enables us to walk around with our head low, but our eyes aimed high. When we believe we are worthless, we are unable to kneel down to help others. Worthlessness makes us lay prostrate and wallow in despair, while humility allows us to kneel down to help others stand. That's why it's important to have friends and family around to help you decipher these differences when we are unable to by ourselves.

Just a brief FYI: not a single one of you reading this is worthless. That is a lie straight from the pit of hell, and you must not grant it access into your heart. You were designed and created with a magnificent purpose. I believe in you. Greatness, not worthlessness, was woven into the fibers of your DNA.

### Comparatively Foolish

One last point I want to make in regards to the subject of humility verses pride, is the want or need to compare yourself with others. This is jealousy, and like pride, it does not foster an atmosphere of being humble. This is a big issue for most of us if we are being honest. Men, by their very nature, are competitive creatures. We want to be the best at everything. When we are not, we feel a great sense of inadequacy. We wrestle internally with the baggage of thoughts like: "How come I don't have that kind of position at my job?" "Why aren't I making that much money?" "I work just as hard as he does." "I wish my house was as big as his." "Geez, I want a new truck too." "God, look at the size of his television!"

And if we're truly being transparent, there are even deeper issues we never vocalize such as: "Why aren't my kids as well behaved?" "Why isn't my wife as pretty as his?" "I wish my family looked at me the way his looks at him." So on and so forth.

We create schemes to accumulate things that really have nothing to do in defining our quality as a man. We silently agonize and suffer by comparison. We are trying to achieve a standard that in the end only promotes either pride or worthlessness. It is shallow at best. Men, we ought to be grateful and humbled by what we do have. When we are humble, we will be lifted up and promoted at the proper time.

> "We do not dare to classify or compare ourselves with some who commend themselves. When they measure themselves by themselves and compare themselves with themselves, they are not wise."

> 2 Corinthians 10:12[10] NIV

We are not using wisdom when we compare ourselves to others. These pissing contests we compete in are meaningless. This comparing and contrasting causes us to be motivated by pride which is diametrically opposed to humility. The man who can appreciatively examine all that he has, all that he has worked for, and all that he holds precious, that is a man with a humble disposition.

It isn't the achievements, or material possessions that make the man. It is the quality of his heart that is reflected onto the world that is the truest measure of his character. There is a vulnerability in humility that we need. Being vulnerable is not the same as being weak. It is not the same as perceived self-worthlessness either. It is being secure in who you are, and not what possessions you own. Author Rick Warren hit the nail on the head by saying, "Humility is not thinking less of yourself, it's thinking of yourself less."[11]

This is exactly right. If you want to be successful, first determine what success means for you. Is it the big house, high paying powerful job, with a trophy wife, and perfect children driving around in luxury cars? If it is, *great!* Go for it! Or is it the respect, love, and admiration of your friends, family, and those who are in your sphere of influence? It is possible to have both, but is it possible to have both and remain humble? That is the question. In 2018 Dwayne "The Rock" Johnson was one of the highest paid actors in the world. Here's what he has to say about success, "I'm always asked, 'What's the secret to success?' But there are no secrets. Be humble. Be hungry. And always be the hardest worker in the room."[12]

Humility is one of the most valuable qualities you can possess as a man. This is what we should want to display for our children, and have them emulate. This is the quality that will make our wives drawn to us and respect us. We need not boast of our achievements, or herald them for the world to see. When we walk in humility, those things will naturally become known to the world. Football coach John Madden sums it up very matter-of-factly: "Self-praise is for losers. Be a winner. Stand for something. Always have class, and be humble."[13]

What I have learned in my life is the more a man has struggled to achieve, the less he talks about it. He just lets the fruits of his labor speak for themself. When a man knows that he has lead a life filled with extraordinary accomplishments, yet feels no compulsion to boast of them, that is when you know a man walks in humility. That man, has slayed the beast of pride, and walks with his head low, and his eyes aimed high. Basketball coach John Wooden said:

> "Talent is God-given. Be humble.
> Fame is man-given. Be grateful.
> Conceit is self-given. Be careful."[14]

# Chapter 11
## Forgiveness

**forgive** / *verb* /  "to grant pardon for or remission of (an offense, debt, etc.); absolve."[1]

The quality of forgiveness may be the most difficult to practically apply in our lives. It could be because we cannot grasp the concept, do not know how, or just flat out refuse to forgive. We believe that if we hold on to that pain or offense committed against us, or those we love, and withhold forgiveness, that we have power over our offenders. In actuality, they are the ones that remain in control over us. Unforgiveness is a cruel master, manipulating us as an marionette while we remain the puppet on the string.

It's like the old Elton John song, *Sorry Seems To Be The Hardest Word*. Becoming fixated on enacting revenge, dishing out punishment, and inflicting pain onto those who have committed these wrongdoings devours your time, energy, and creativity. Preoccupation with the relentless questioning of "how?' and "why?' whatever wrongs occurred, robs you of so much.

A heart without forgiveness is one that navigates life by looking backwards, not forward. You see, my friends, forgiveness is a two-way street, and it is one that can only be traveled on by the strong, and wise. There will be times in life when we must forgive, as well as ask for forgiveness. Which is rarely, if ever, easy. Mahatma Gandhi once observed that, "The weak can never forgive. Forgiveness is the attribute of the strong."[2]

In this chapter, we will be discussing the aspects of giving and asking for forgiveness. Additionally, we will be examining an often-overlooked area of unforgiveness that unquestionably yields the most dangerous consequences. So as we begin, let's be open and honest with ourselves. Who do we need to forgive? Why do we need to forgive them? And how can we forgive them? Bruce Lee once said, "Mistakes are always forgivable, if one has the courage to admit them."[3]

## The Pope Tenet

Poet Alexander Pope famously stated, "To err is human; to forgive, divine"[4] We humans, men particularly, have a gift for screwing up in the most spectacular of ways. Forgiveness is a quality directly from God himself. A concept surely we could not have figured out without a nudge from The Almighty. If we agree, that forgiveness is a quality that is divine in nature; we must also agree that it is a quality that we should reciprocate likewise. Consider this:

"If we confess our sins, he is faithful and just and will forgive us our sins and purify us from all unrighteousness."

1 John 1:9[5] NIV

What we see is a cause and effect that is the crux of the forgiveness dilemma. We have to first recognize the need for forgiveness, and then ask for it. Whether you call this confession, or owning up to your mistakes, you must first acknowledge that you did something you ought not have done. That undoubtedly is the most challenging part. The first step is always the most difficult. The beautiful thing is that once you ask God for forgiveness, He does. You get a clean slate. In fact, the Scriptures says this about the extent of His forgiveness:

"as far as the east is from the west, so far has he removed our transgressions from us."

Psalm 103:12[6] NIV

Forgiveness is extended to us from the sacrificial act Jesus performed on the cross. This is how we are forgiven, and why we should forgive others. The lengths Jesus went through to demonstrate His willingness to forgive, is what makes it possible for us to forgive. When we ask Him to forgive us, He does, and then He takes those mistakes and removes them far from us. Like I mentioned before, forgiveness is a two-way street. This is how forgiveness works: you have to give it so you can receive it. Jesus talked about the law of reciprocity otherwise known as the law of the harvest, which states:

"A man reaps what he sows."

Galatians 6:7b[7] NIV

I want to elaborate on the philosophy of reaping and sowing because it's as applicable to matters of the heart as it is to the physical world in which we live. We have to forgive, as we have been forgiven. Just as we must ask for forgiveness, we need to also forgive those who have trespassed against us. It operates much in the same manner as respect. You have to show respect in order to be respected; it isn't automatically given. Comprehending this is of the utmost importance.

Forgiveness is a tough business. Which is precisely why a lot of people don't enter into it. The capitol needed to fund it is benevolence and wisdom. Humility is ultimately the quality that allows us the ability to forgive. We have to count the cost and evaluate the profit that will either be lost or gained by the decision to extend or withhold. You must be honest in order to accept and extend forgiveness. Author Brennan Manning words it excellently, " Sin and forgiveness and falling and getting back up and losing the pearl of great price in the couch cushions but then finding it again, and again, and again? Those are the stumbling steps to becoming Real, the only script that's really worth following in this world or the one that's coming."[8] When we can confess that we were truly injured by someone else, we can then begin to move towards genuinely asking and giving forgiveness.

### Forgiving, "Them..."

I struggle with forgiveness. I sincerely do. This is something that I am working out in my life, as I trust you are as well. However, what we fail to realize is that we grant those individuals power over us, and the wounds will never heal, as long as we harbor ill will and unforgiveness in our hearts. Actor Tyler Perry said, "The most important thing that I learned in growing up is that forgiveness is something that, when you do it, you free yourself to move on."[9] Unforgiveness is a prison that we willingly keep ourselves in. We neglect to realize that we hold the key to our own freedom. Refusing forgiveness to those who have hurt us doesn't cause injury to others, only ourselves.

What you sow, you will reap. There is duality, and an additional benefit to forgiveness. When you forgive, you can be forgiven in return. Unless you can forgive others, you can not be forgiven. This is a concept that isn't taught on too much. The scripture says:

"14 If you forgive those who sin against you, your heavenly Father will forgive you.
15 But if you refuse to forgive others, your Father will not forgive your sins."

Matthew 6:14-15[10 NLT]

We must forgive, so we can be forgiven in return. I know I keep harping on this, but we must have this concept woven into our garments of manliness. I personally think being able to forgive others does make it easier for us to accept forgiveness too. Yet, as it stands, if you sow unforgiveness, you cannot reap forgiveness. It's like sowing tomato seeds, and expecting to reap cucumbers. It just doesn't work that way. Furthermore:

"This is how I want you to conduct yourself in these matters. If you enter your place of worship and, about to make an offering, you suddenly remember a grudge a friend has against you, abandon your offering, leave immediately, go to this friend and make things right. Then and only then, come back and work things out with God."

Matthew 5:23-24[11 MSG]

In my opinion, this is quite possibly the most frightening thing about unforgiveness. We need The Father to forgive us, but He cannot unless we forgive those who have done us wrong. The very notion that we can't even begin to work things out with Him should be absolutely disconcerting to us.

Perhaps the person who hurt you the deepest is not available for you to speak to directly. It could be that they are not alive anymore, or that there is just no way to contact them. Even if there is no possible way to communicate with them directly, you still must forgive them. I know this is easier said than done, but you can do it. Once you do, it will become uncomplicated. I promise. Once you experience forgiveness, you can offer it to others more easily than you ever could have before. I like how Pastor Rick Warren words it, "You know, when you've experienced grace and you feel like you've been forgiven, you're a lot more forgiving of other people. You're a lot more gracious to others."[12] I know it's hard. It's hard to admit we're wrong. It's hard to admit that someone actually got close enough to hurt us. Trust me, I know. But until you begin to forgive, you won't be forgiven, nor will you be truly free from the person or persons that brought this agony upon you in the first place.

Occasionally—I would wager more often than not—when we are hurt, the person or persons that hurt us have no idea what they've done. They could sincerely be ignorant of the impact of their words or deeds. If this is the case, we have to approach them with humility. I don't care who you are, it is never easy to tell someone, "You hurt me." Be that as it may, how else will they know, and how else can we forgive them, unless we mention it? No one has the ability to read your mind. Look at this verse:

> "Be alert. If you see your friend going wrong, correct him. If he responds, forgive him. Even if it's personal against you and repeated seven times through the day, and seven times he says, 'I'm sorry, I won't do it again,' forgive him."

> Luke 17:3-4[13] MSG

Now don't be a jerk about it. Most likely this is gong to be as uncomfortable for them as it is for you. Using your own words, try to convey this sentiment, "This really hurt me when you said or did this. I just wanted to let you know that I forgive you." Now, hopefully, this will go well, and they will respond in kind, At this point, feel free to hug it out, fist bump, shake hands, or whatever expression of reconciliation seems most appropriate (*and of course manly*) to you both. I bet right now you're asking yourself, "What if they keep hurting me over and over again?" Might I suggest this:

> "At that point Peter got up the nerve to ask, "Master, how many times do I forgive a brother or sister who hurts me? Seven?" Jesus replied, "Seven! Hardly. Try seventy times seven."

> Matthew 18:21-22[11] MSG

There are a few things you should know concerning the above verse. If you are the one that is approaching the person who has committed the offense, please be as sensitive as possible. That doesn't mean beat around the bush. Be sincere, and speak your mind with wisdom and benevolence. Try not to be an ass or lord their mistake over them. Whatever you do, don't be cocky when bringing these things up. I guarantee that will not improve the situation. Be polite, attentive, and hear them out. Be a man. Apply the qualities that you have been honing throughout our quest together.

We are to continually forgive, no matter what. If someone keeps doing the same boneheaded things to you all the time, you still have to forgive them. Know this though: forgiving doesn't mean you have to forget. Look at it this way; it's a consolidation process. Essentially, they are helping you to narrow down the people that should be granted access into your heart. If the same thing is repeatedly happening from the same person, you most likely deserve the pain they are causing you. You may ask, "How can you say that?" Simple, I firmly believe you deserve what you tolerate. Forgiving while not forgetting is part of the process to obtaining wisdom. If you remember how, and in this case who, was the source of the pain, chances are you will remember in the future to avoid these circumstances when dealing with these individuals.

If you are the one being approached with a legitimate issue, don't react, respond. When an individual whom you know, especially someone you hold in high esteem, brings a genuine grievance to you, don't react poorly. Listen with an open mind, and evaluate your heart to see if there is any validity to the claim. I word it that way because sometimes people will be offended far too easily. Those people may just want to create drama. You need not bow down to this kind of behavior if that is indeed the case. However, be humble either way. If the offense does carry merit, be man enough to admit you were wrong and apologize.

So, what if it doesn't go as well as what you wanted it to? It is possible that it won't. You should always hope for the best, yet prepare for the worst. If that is the predicament you find yourself in, and it doesn't turn out as you had hoped, keep this in mind…

"Never pay back evil with more evil. Do things in such a way that everyone can see you are honorable. Do all that you can to live in peace with everyone.
Dear friends, never take revenge. Leave that to the righteous anger of God.
For the Scriptures say, "I will take revenge; I will pay them back," says the Lord.
Instead, "If your enemies are hungry, feed them. If they are thirsty, give them something to drink.
In doing this, you will heap burning coals of shame on their heads." Don't let evil conquer you, but conquer evil by doing good."

Romans 12:17-21[14] NLT

Playwright Oscar Wilde summarizes the sentiment by saying,

"Always forgive your enemies — nothing annoys them so much."[15] This approach takes some time and practice to master. If you are pretending to extend forgiveness because it pisses someone off, that's merely revenge masquerading as forgiveness. When you sincerely forgive those who have committed wrong against you, it throws them off guard. They would expect you to retaliate. However, treating them kindly and walking with genuine forgiveness in your heart annoys them all the more. This becomes disarming, and allows for their motives to be exposed. Don't delight in that too much, for we will at some point and time not only be on the giving, but receiving end of this.

If you doubt that you possess ability to forgive, remember: Jesus was spat on, beaten, and forced to carry his own cross to his death site. Yet He chose to forgive. We are also capable of this same kind of forgiveness. Forgiveness isn't easy, but it is simple.

### Forgiving, "Me...?"

Earlier, I mentioned that there's an overlooked aspect to forgiveness that we must address. Which is simply this: the one person that most people can never seem to forgive is themself. That same struggle lies within me, as well as those men whom I have studied and admired throughout my life. This is often a neglected facet of forgiveness, seldom talked about in most circles of culture. This has to change, and in order to do so, we must confront it head on. Writer Lewis B. Smedes explains, "To forgive is to set a prisoner free and discover that the prisoner was you."[16]

Entertainer Mark Wahlberg had extensive legal issues as a young man including narcotics trafficking, drug abuse, assault, and even attempted murder. He was able to turn his life around by understanding the process of forgiving others, as well as yourself. He said, "I did a lot of things that I regretted and I certainly paid for my mistakes. You have to go and ask for forgiveness and it wasn't until I really started doing good and doing right, by other people as well as myself, that I really started to feel that guilt go away. So I don't have a problem going to sleep at night."[17]

One of the most difficult lessons I ever had to learn was to forgive myself for the mistakes I've made. I have been truly disappointed and infuriated with myself at times. I find it relatively easier by comparison to forgive others than myself. Even though God has forgiven me, I wrestle to find any plausible reason for me to do the same. After all, I am the one who caused all this pain. I thought I deserved to be miserable, that my penance was beating myself up. I thought that in some kind of sick, twisted way that the agony I was putting myself through would somehow satisfy some debt that I owed.

Professional wrestler Lex Luger spoke on the importance of forgiving yourself. He said, "Many times, the decisions we make affect and hurt your closest friends and family the most. I have a lot of regrets in that regard. But God has forgiven me, which I am very thankful for. It has enabled me to forgive myself and move forward one day at a time."[18] Forgiving everyone but ourselves, is really a dangerous thing. Often we don't even consider that it is even needed. We believe that we deserve to be punished, and withholding forgiveness is just the most subversive way we can do this to ourselves.

Gentlemen, it is alright to forgive yourself. Actually, you must before you can truly understand and appreciate the divinity and the quality that is beheld in forgiveness. I want to say this to you personally and directly: you have permission to forgive yourself.

If you need the words to do so, maybe start here: "I forgive myself. I admit I messed up, and I will do my best to not do that again. I am worth being forgiven. I am only human, and I will not harbor unforgiveness towards myself any longer."

I am aware of the delicate subject this is. In life bad stuff happens. Stuff that is not so easily forgotten or gotten over. Stuff that has no logical reason for occurring. People suck, situations are tragic, and like my mother used to tell me, "Life ain't always fair." This is not to belittle the severity of the hardships we all endure. These facts are not new to many of us. However, the ability to identify and then act on the need to forgive may be. Radio Host Bernard Meltzer said, " When you forgive, you in no way change the past — but you sure do change the future."[19]

We must find the courage to forgive. The capability and the capacity are within you. Yes, the hurt is real. Yes, the mistakes you made may not be as easily erased as just saying you're sorry. Yes, other people may have done unthinkably horrendous things to you. Yes, I know it's hard to forgive, especially when every fiber in your being is screaming out not to. Yes, I know that some may have no clue what they have done to you. I challenge you to forgive them nonetheless.

Dr. Kent Keith wrote "The Paradoxical Commandments," and although he did not explicitly use the word "forgive," at its core lies the elements of forgiveness.

> "People are illogical, unreasonable, and self-centered.
> Love them anyway.

If you do good, people will accuse you of selfish ulterior motives.
Do good anyway.

If you are successful, you will win false friends and true enemies.
Succeed anyway.

The good you do today will be forgotten tomorrow.
Do good anyway.

Honesty and frankness make you vulnerable.
Be honest and frank anyway.

The biggest men and women with the biggest ideas can be shot down by the smallest                    men and women with the smallest minds.
Think big anyway.

People favor underdogs but follow only top dogs.
Fight for a few underdogs anyway.

What you spend years building may be destroyed overnight.
Build anyway.

People really need help but may attack you if you do help them.
Help people anyway.

Give the world the best you have and you'll get kicked in the teeth.
Give the world the best you have anyway."[20]

# Chapter 12
## Accountability And Loyalty

**accountability** / *noun* / "the state of being accountable, liable, or answerable."[1]

**accountable** / *adjective* / "1. subject to the obligation to report, explain, or justify something; responsible; answerable. 2. capable of being explained; explicable; explainable."[2]

**loyalty** / *noun* / "the state or quality of being loyal; faithfulness to commitments or obligations."[3]

Gentlemen, the ties that bind together all of the qualities we have discussed thus far are accountability and loyalty. U2 was correct to say that *Sometimes You Can't Make It On Your Own*. Rarely, if ever, can anyone make a go of anything by themselves and have any measurable amount of success. The fallacy we buy into is that we do not need anyone's help, counsel, or (*dare I say it?*) shoulder to cry on. The foolish notion of the self-made man, has unfortunately taken hold in our culture. A loner mentality creates a slippery slope that usually ends up yielding hazardous results.

It is no surprise that most men in America are seemingly isolated. Sure we pretend we have companionship, however in reality our "Band of Brothers" typically just amounts to an "Army of One."

Many men I know tend to believe there is a great deal of difficulty in finding other men that you can confide in. Perhaps a distinction of our relationships must be made. I do know a lot of people I would label as an acquaintance, but a friend? No.

So why is that? Dr. Todd Kashdan, from an article in *Psychology Today* entitled "Why Do Men Have a Hard Time Making Friends?" offers one plausible explanation, "Ask school children who their friends are and many list last names close to them in the alphabet. Why? Because most friendships are determined by seating charts. Schools shove future friends in your face. During the innocence of youth, proximity alone is grounds for liking someone. But things change dramatically as we get older, especially for men. Open-mindedness takes a hit. What other people think of us and where we stand in the social hierarchy is of epic importance. But there's something else that makes it hard to make friends, something insidious that few people talk about."

Kashdan continues, "When men hit their 30's, many cling to their high school and college friends. And if these don't last, men have a hard time forming new friendships. I'm not talking about work-out partners and neighbors you pound a few beers with while ribs are grilling, I'm talking about confidants. People who you are willing to share your innermost self to because you feel it will be valued and accepted (regardless of what evils lurk there). Women are fantastic at cultivating these relationships. Women spend substantial time and energy to creating intimate relationships, safe havens, and people that care about the good things that happen to them. Men? Not so much."[4]

This is something that I can identify with completely. I have known my closest friends nearly my entire life. There is a comfort, and acceptable level of embarrassment and harassment, that comes along with these relationships. They've seen you at your best, been there for you at your worst, and vice versa. There is an assuredness that comes with sharing time and experiences that transcends all other societal bonds. Yet the question lingers: are you accountable to these men? Are they the confidants that Dr. Kashdan refers to?

## Secure Vulnerability

What do I mean when I say accountability? It's simple. You find someone that you can be authentic, and unguarded with, and he reciprocates those same sentiments towards you. Then you share with each other the things you want to improve upon in your life. "That is a tall order, Bill," you may be saying. To that end, I agree. You don't just find that kind of guy on every corner in town. There is a careful vetting process that must occur to find someone that you can trust to hold you, and be held, to account. When we can hold and be held accountable we will be put in a place to be vulnerable. Which is good. That's the entire point. Dr. Tom Price puts it like this, "One person's embarrassment is another person's accountability."[5]

This is nothing to be dismissive towards. We have struggles we cannot bear on our own. We have addictions and weaknesses, that will overtake us if we do not have someone to watch our back. They will inhabit our hearts and minds while pursuing us with reckless abandon. Which is precisely why it is a necessity to have a partner to help shine a light in to our darkness, and go into battle with us. And during their hour of need. likewise, we hold fast to those oaths we have taken. The Bible places a high value on the bonds made between men:

"As iron sharpens iron, So one man sharpens [and influences] another [through discussion]."
Proverbs 27:17[6] AMP

Accountability is never easy. This is why the feeble and foolish dismiss such notions. Men being open and transparent with themselves is a near Herculean task. Keep these two things in mind once you have begun to be accountable to someone: First, when you start to become accountable, it is awkward and constrictive. Second, you have to realize right off the bat that you will not always see eye to eye, but that you don't need to either. From time to time you aren't going to like what your accountability partner will have to say, and vice versa; that is, if it's being done correctly. Holding and being held to account is messy business dealing with the unseen parts of other men's lives. The aforementioned verse is a perfect description of how, when done properly, it should look.

I own an axe and when I first got it, it was incredibly sharp, but after I had used it for a while, it became dull. I have sharpened lots of knives before, but never an axe. I assume one would perform that task in a similar fashion, but it didn't seem to be as effective. I asked my dad how to put a new edge on it, and he showed me. He took the axe, turned on the grinder, ran it past the wheel a few times and proceeded to make it just like new. It was so sharp you could shave the hair right off your back. However, I observed something while he was sharpening the axe: sparks went flying everywhere. This is a perfect analogy for what accountability will often look like. When we decide to become accountable, sparks often will fly.

When we have someone we trust to protect our secrets and internal conflicts, a bond develops that is unlike any other relationship that you will have. When you confess issues such as you have an addiction to pornography, you can't seem to put the bottle down, or you are not the father you know that you can be, these are not the type of things that everyone should be privileged to. You can't tell the guy that owns the local cigar shop who you see occasionally that you're abusive towards your wife or girlfriend. That your boss keeps on approaching you about "working late hours" and taking a "long weekend business trip," or that you gambled away your retirement fund. Maybe your point of contention isn't as severe as those. Maybe the big controversies in your life are that you play video games too often and neglect your work or personal life. Perhaps you are depressed, and can't seem to get off the couch. Maybe you eat too much. Whatever the issue, we need someone to encourage us to stay on track and hold our feet to the fire when necessary. The scriptures recommend this:

> "Make this your common practice: Confess your sins to each other and pray for each other so that you can live together whole and healed. The prayer of a person living right with God is something powerful to be reckoned with."

> James 5:16[7] MSG

As they say, confession is good for the soul. When we are accountable to one another, healing can come into our lives. We can again walk that narrow path. This is a wonderful gift to be given. We can be healed and released from these corrosive elements that plague us from becoming the man we were intended, and whom our hearts have longed to be. And when we wander from the righteous path we committed ourselves to, it is in the safety of accountability under the watchful and loving eye of a trusted friend who will help guide our way back to true north.

In my life, I have a select few men who keep me accountable, and I them. It has taken a long time to develop the trust that we have in one another, and it hasn't all been a bed of roses. I have said those hard things to them, and they to me. There has been tears, laughter, and arguments. The reason we put up with each other's crap is because, we have decided that there is value in one another.

If I may offer some wisdom while selecting the men to be accountable with, it would be: don't pick a "Yes-Man." For as surely as you are reading this, no benefit will befall upon you. The gentlemen that perpetually says "yes" or agrees with everything you say and do will watch you walk off the cliff and say it's the best decision you could have ever made. The best man for the job has the ability to stay on you, and possesses the will to call you out when needed. The same goes for someone asking you to hold him accountable. If you can't tell him the truth when he needs to hear it, decline the offer. It will profit you both in the long run.

It is a great honor and responsibility to be granted access into the inner courts of another man's heart and mind. It is a task not to be taken lightly. It is a relationship, which, if nurtured properly, will be an effective catalyst for consistency in the quality of man you become. Businessman Stephen Covey puts it, "Accountability breeds response-ability."[8]

## I Got Your Six

Now that we have established a need for men to be accountable to one another, let's examine why this isn't happening as frequently as it should be. Men tend to have more casual relationships than formal friendships, Acquaintances cannot provide the transparency and vulnerability to foster any substantial benefits like holding one another responsible in word and deed. Personally, I identify the problem as a deficiency in loyalty. From what I have experienced and witnessed from other men, it all boils down to the fact that they simply cannot trust anyone enough to be vulnerable, therefore they can't begin to be accountable. Many men fear being accountable because of the susceptibility that comes with it. And since a lot of us have never had anyone show us much as far as loyalty is concerned, we avoid these types of relationships like the plague.

Sadly, and for reasons I can't quite explain, men that remain loyal to each other are as rare as Sasquatch dung. You find that men who are in teams are loyal, but this has to be taught and fostered in the right kind of atmosphere. Whether it is those who serve together in the military, first responders, or teammates, these are all positions that do not flourish under the auspices of individual reliance. People who enter into these arenas know that their success is solely dependent upon being able to trust that the dude next to them has their six. Baseball player Ernie Banks put it. "Loyalty and friendship, which is to me the same, created all the wealth that I've ever thought I'd have." [9]

Disloyalty amongst men and their closest confidants has been morosely established. Whether historical accounts or other references, there are many examples for us to learn from: Billy the Kid and Pat Garrett, Snowflake and Napoleon, Julius Caesar and Brutus, Jesus Christ and Judas. Let's see what the scriptures say about friendship and loyalty:

"A friend is always loyal, and a brother is born to help in time of need."

Proverbs 17:17 [10] NLT

Ideas like loyalty and allegiance, seem antiquated today. Self-centeredness is what takes precedence. That is what is being pushed upon us. Those modern thoughts are a poop-flavored lollypop presented in a 24 karat gold wrapper. It isn't something's packaging that gives it value; it is the item itself. If the component is useless, it doesn't matter how beautifully presented it is. True evil is about betrayal, and once that package has enticed you to open it there is a world full of hurt awaiting you.

A stalwart man is not swayed by fashion. He remains steadfast and resolute, even if the world and all around him does not. The idea of being a loyal and trustworthy man is an ageless quality. So… how do you become loyal? And likewise, how can you determine if someone isn't worthy of your loyalty?

To answer the first question, how do I become loyal? I will let Baseball Coach Tommy Lasorda answer that, "You give loyalty, you'll get it back. You give love, you'll get it back."[11] When you are loyal, people will be loyal to you in return. Have you ever had a boss that stuck their neck out for you? Chances are they were trying to be loyal. As a result, I would wager that you were more apt to be a better and increasingly more loyal employee in return. Loyalty breeds and attracts loyalty, just as the case for the other qualities we have discussed on our quest. This is a prime example of the law of the harvest. Be loyal first, people will either follow suit or not. It will be easily detectable.

Second question, how can I determine if someone isn't going to be loyal? This is not as hard to answer as you may think. Here is an unfortunate truth told to us by General James "Mad Dog" Mattis,

"Treachery has existed as long as there's been warfare, and there's always been a few people that you couldn't trust."[12] If we keep in mind there have always been those who can't be trusted, that makes recognizing them all the easier. You see, those not worthy of our trust, will just betray us. I do not know of any other way to detect with 100% accuracy. Sure your gut may tell you something, but the distrustful will always he the one holding the knife inserted in your back.

The deepest cuts typically comes from those closest to us. This is one of the many records wisdom plays us from her collection. Wrestler John Cena said, "When people show loyalty to you, you take care of those who are with you. It's how it goes with everything. If you have a small circle of friends, and one of those friends doesn't stay loyal to you, they don't stay your friend for very long."[13]

### Owning Up

The last thing I want to mention is personal accountability. We have to begin owning up to our mistakes and be accountable and responsible for our decisions and the consequences thereof. Actor Stephen Baldwin said, "I learned in an extremely hard way that the accountability falls with me."[14] The Bible is very clear on this:

"So then, each of us will give an account of ourselves to God."

Romans 14:12[15] NIV

The concept of averting accountability and shirking our responsibilities is extremely prevalent today. I see many men, dodging blame and pointing fingers at others. The man that has fully comprehended the qualities within these pages, would never do that. Baseball player Herschel Walker commented, "That person has to be accountable for himself. I think that's what we have to do in society today is to be accountable for yourself."[16]

Taking ownership of our mistakes isn't an automatic admission of guilt. It is, however, a part of the developmental process of life and becoming a man. Blaming others, instead of being accountable for what we have done, is cowardice—pure and simple. Could it be that we are individually responsible for the choices we make, and need to be held to account as a result? Accountability is a much-needed quality that has to be reestablished in our time. As men, we must raise a standard and be the one to set the example. We must decide that we will not only be personably accountable, put we will be held to account by others for our mistakes.

I encourage you to be a man who is continually accountable and loyal. You will ultimately attract those kinds of gentlemen to yourself. It is a process that takes time, as well as some trial and error. I guarantee it will be worthwhile for you in the future. Not every man is decent or capable enough for you to make this kind of oath with. And not every man is going to be responsible for the decisions they make. Some men just have too much damage from past betrayals, with burdens too heavy and pains too deep, that they are unable to be placed in that position. Some men are chicken-hearted and will not own up to their choices. Do your best to help if you can, but be mindful nonetheless.

Bear this in mind: all of the characteristics we have gone over are all for naught if we do not grasp these concepts. It is the quality to become accountable and loyal that will define you as a man. Seek to find men who will lift you up and assist you, as you will for them along your quest. We cannot do this on our own. It's a fact. Most men don't have the willpower or strength to hold their own feet to the flame when the shadow of adversity encroaches upon them. This is why we have brothers that will love us enough to hold them there with us. It is this very revelation that Zach Galifianakis shares in *The Hangover* when he speaks about his wolf pack.

"You guys might not know this, but I consider myself a bit of a loner. I tend to think of myself as a one-man wolf pack. But when my sister brought Doug home, I knew he was one of my own. And my wolf pack... it grew by one. So there... there were two of us in the wolf pack... I was alone first in the pack, and then Doug joined in later. And six months ago, when Doug introduced me to you guys, I thought, 'Wait a second, could it be?' And now I know for sure, I just added two more guys to my wolf pack. Four of us wolves, running around the desert together, in Las Vegas, looking for strippers and cocaine."[17]

# Parting Shots

Gentlemen, while our time together on this journey may be concluding, our quest has just begun. We have only started to rediscover and reclaim the fundamental essences of who we are as men. I am grateful that you have sojourned with me thus far, and if you will indulge me just a while longer, I have some final thoughts to share with you...

The body of this book was originally written between September to November 2016. It came to me very quickly and supernaturally, I would say Divinely. It was a very stormy, and turbulent time for our culture and society, the likes we've never seen before. Little did I know, the most devastating storm of my life was brewing just off my shores, and out of my peripheral view.

My wife of fourteen years left me, and we are now divorced. This completely caught me off guard and I have spent the time from then to now reconciling with my loss, and pain, whilst grappling with the contents of this book. I have felt alone, afraid, and confused. The days following her departure were the darkest I have ever known, and I would never wish that kind of torment on anyone.

I share this not to drag her through the mud, or to have any fingers pointed. Truth is, without her, I may not have made it through many of the obstacles I faced during our years together. I want the absolute best for her. I hope and pray that she finds true contentment. I only regret that I could not give that to her. Divorce is a messy, vile thing and it takes its toll on all involved and leaves a wake of devastation in its path. I am not so different than many of you men out there. I've lived, loved, and failed.

I only mention this because, like so many men who have faced adversity, it becomes so easy to discount ourselves and become deceived that we have no value. This has been my journey. It's embarrassing and hurtful but if you can glean any kind of wisdom from my experience than it was not all in vain.

I've cried, trembled, raged, and doubted the man whose eye glared back into mine. I've confronted, confessed, conceded, and eventually coalesced with him. Not unscathed, but more assured of whose, and whom I am.

I struggle with the fact that I, and the subject matter of this book, was hypocritical and deceitful. That I didn't have the slightest idea of what I was talking about. How dare I even try to expound on such a subject. That I'm a charlatan. That I have no authority, or right to be helping anyone else, when I had lost the single most valuable relationship this side of Heaven I had ever had.

I strived so hard to be the proper example of a man. After she left I was convinced I was the furthest thing from. Yet so many friends asked me about this project, of which I had all but completely given up on. So I unearthed these pages and slowly began to realize I am that man. That, at moments unbeknownst to me, these qualities I had clung to and they saw me through… That they were in me all the while, and I believe they are within you too.

I understand the fear we face when confronted by things we know nothing about or that leave us disheartened. When we are surrounded by circumstances that we are unfamiliar with, we tend to get frustrated and quit. When men feel incompetent at something, chances are they give up. From my experience, in those moments we either blow up, bail, or want to pound the hell out of something (*often all three*). We tend to quit prematurely, or get bitter rather than better. However, don't give up on trying to implement these qualities into your life. It is all a part of the objectives assigned to us on our quest. We crave challenges and opportunities to put ourselves to the test. To see what we are made of.

Do not allow your progress to be halted and stop you from moving forward. Continue to mature and develop, refuse to stay stuck in a proverbial rut. In order to be all that we were created to be, we have to evolve from a boy to a man. Have you ever heard the old adage, "what isn't growing is dying?" Same with us men. When we become less focused on the pageantry of our outward appearance and performance, we can refocus our attention on how to allow our heart to heal and develop those qualities that bring inward benefits that effect our entire being. What we allow to ripen inside of us as we grow, will overflow and overtake everything in and out of us, be it good or bad.

The mark we ought to be aiming for is encapsulated below:

> "Summing it all up, friends, I'd say you'll do best by filling your minds and meditating on things true, noble, reputable, authentic, compelling, gracious—the best, not the worst; the beautiful, not the ugly; things to praise, not things to curse."
>
> Philippians 4:8[1] MSG

As a man you are NOT defined by your job, material possessions, financial portfolios, or the gifts and skills you have acquired. All of he educational achievements, sexual conquests, fights you have fought, victories you have won, and battles you have lost, do NOT determine who you are. The accolades and awards you have amassed should NOT necessarily describe anything about you. You ARE defined by the qualities you possess and display. Oftentimes, we become far too focused on how we present the outer-man, while we've neglected to see that our inner-man has slowly been withering away. Take comfort in this:

> "For we all stumble *and* sin in many *ways*. If anyone does not stumble in what he says [never saying the wrong thing], he is a perfect man [fully developed in character, without serious flaws], able to bridle his whole body *and* rein in his entire nature [taming his human faults and weaknesses]."
>
> James 3:2[2 AMP]

We all have shortcomings. We all have a unique set of problems that if gone unmanaged, will consume and destroy us. If we permit that to happen we will be robbing the people in our lives, and the world, of all we have to offer. I love what Actor Kevin Costner said in *Man of Steel*. In the most poignant moment in the entire film, Jonathan Kent says to his son Clark, "You just have to decide what kind of a man you want to grow up to be, Clark; because whoever that man is, good character or bad, he's... He's gonna change the world."[3]

In the Spiderman mythology, the pivotal moment that determines the entire course of Peter Parker's destiny is contained within one sentence. Peter's Uncle, Ben, tells him, "Remember, with great power comes great responsibility."[4] This rings equally true for us.

Now that we have read, and understood some of what man's missing attributes are, you are held to account for this information. Sorry, not sorry. We know what we ought to do, we have the power and the responsibility to be resolute. To be held to account, called to task with becoming as authentic as we possibly can.

As this is both daunting and challenging, just keep in mind that you will not be alone on your quest. As for myself, this book has reinforced the fact that I must stay the course. I have to keep my compass pointed to true north and press on. I humbly ask that you join me. Together, we can reach our world and make it a better place. We can influence, and instruct those we love and have sway over. I believe in you. You can accomplish your goals. You are a man of great importance who no longer is unaware of the fact that he has the ability to impact his culture in the most profoundly positive and constructive ways. I present you with this charge:

> "Be watchful, stand firm in the faith, act like men, be strong.
> Let all that you do be done in love."

1 Corinthians 16:13-14[5] ESV

Every man is the lead character in his own life story. Whether you are the protagonist or antagonist, the choice is yours. You and you alone can make your life count for something. To lead a life completely and utterly worthwhile that yields the maximum results from your toils and troubles. You only live once. Endure the trials and tribulations that come your way and do your best to leave this world a little better than you found it. I mean you're going to have to go through some difficult crap anyway, might as well make it count. I love what Author Hunter S. Thompson said, "Life should not be a journey to the grave with the intention of arriving safely in a pretty and well preserved body, but rather to skid in broadside in a cloud of smoke, thoroughly used up, totally worn out, and loudly proclaiming "Wow! What a Ride!"[6]

### Vaya Con Dios

This is my parting shot: walk with your head down and your eyes high. Carry yourself as men. The danger of doing nothing is greater than the risk of trying something. Men with honor will often have those less honorable seeking to gain favor and access to their company. Be watchful for beggars and hangers on. Rest assured, though, when the winds of adversity roar, seldom will they stand. Hardships have a tendency to separate men from boys.

Please keep this in mind. Where there's a lack of authenticity, there's a lack of reverence. As you survey the path set before you, always allow these words to accompany you. Perhaps men have been discounted, marginalized, and neutered because we have refused to be authentic with our friends, families, and most grievously, ourselves. We have not allowed the true content of our hearts to be on display, while the messes we made were.

Gentleman, no matter your circumstances, no matter how hard life has beaten you down, YOU HAVE IMMEASURABLE WORTH. You are intrinsically valuable to The Almighty and those who remain a part of your life. You do contribute to society. As long as you are alive, and trying, you are not a loser. You may have lost a few battles but you are far from losing the war.

And with all said and done, I finally leave you with this. Find what is most dear to you and pursue it. Be relentless, passionate, mindful, considerate, but above all: be a man.

"When I was a child, I talked like a child, I thought like a child,
I reasoned like a child.
When I became a man, I put the ways of childhood behind me."

1 Corinthians 13:17 NIV

# Bibliography

## Chapter 0: Greeting and Salutations

[1] 20180, Jeff Poor7 Mar. "Tucker Carlson Warns of 'Something Ominous' Happening to Men in America --- 'Men Seem to Be Becoming Less Male'." *Breitbart*, 8 Mar. 2018, www.breitbart.com/video/2018/03/07/tucker-carlson-warns-something-ominous-happening-men-america-men-seem-becoming-less-male/

## Chapter 1: Definition and Quality

[1] definition. (n.d.). *Dictionary.com Unabridged*. Retrieved September 26, 2016 from Dictionary.com website http://www.dictionary.com/browse/definition

[2] male. (n.d.). *Dictionary.com Unabridged*. Retrieved September 26, 2016 from Dictionary.com website http://www.dictionary.com/browse/male

[3] *Kindergarten Cop*. Dir. Ivan Reitman. Screenplay by Murray Salem. Perf. Arnold Schwarzenegger, Penelope Ann Miller, Pamela Reed. 1990. Film.

[4] man. (n.d.). *Dictionary.com Unabridged*. Retrieved September 26, 2016 from Dictionary.com website http://www.dictionary.com/browse/man

[5] "quality". *Dictionary.com Unabridged*. Random House, Inc. 3 Oct. 2016. <Dictionary.com http://www.dictionary.com/browse/quality>.

[6] *1 Peter. Complete Jewish Bible*. N.p.: David H. Stern, n.d. Web. 1998.

[7] *The Lord of the Rings: The Two Towers*. Dir. Peter Jackson. Screenplay by Fran Walsh, Philippa Boyens, and Steven Sinclair. Prod. Peter Jackson. By J.R.R. Tolkien. Perf. Elijah Wood, Ian McKellen, Viggo Mortensen, Sean Astin, Liv Tyler, John Rhys-Davies, Bernard Hill, Billy Boyd, Dominic Monaghan, Orlando Bloom, Christopher Lee, Robyn Malcolm, Sean Bean, Ian Holm, Andy Serkis. New Line Home Entertainment, 2003. Film.

[8] Roosevelt, Theodore, Jr. "The Man In The Arena." Citizenship in a Republic. France, Paris. 23        Apr. 1910. Speech.

**Chapter 2: Character**

[1] character. (n.d.). *Dictionary.com Unabridged*. Retrieved September 26, 2016 from Dictionary.com website http://www.dictionary.com/browse/character

[2] *1Corinthians. Www.biblegateway.com*. Amplified Bible, Classic Edition )AMPC), n.d. Web. A6 Sept. 2016. <https://www.biblegateway.com/passage/?search=1+Corinthians+15%3A33&version=AMPC>. Amplified Bible, Classic Edition (AMPC) Copyright © 1954, 1958, 1962, 1964, 1965, 1987 by The Lockman Foundation

[3] H. Jackson Brown, Jr.." BrainyQuote.com. Xplore Inc, 2016. 2 December 2016. https://www.brainyquote.com/quotes/quotes/h/hjacksonb101336.ht

[4] *Romans. Romans 5:3-4*. N.p.: n.p., n.d. *BibleGateway.com*. Web. 26 Sept. 2016. New International Version (NIV) Holy Bible, New International Version®, NIV® Copyright ©1973, 1978, 1984, 2011 by Biblica, Inc.® Used by permission. All rights reserved worldwide.

[5] "Les Brown." BrainyQuote.com. Xplore Inc, 2016. 2 December 2016.

https://www.brainyquote.com/quotes/quotes/l/lesbrown636311.html

[6]*Galatians. The Message*. 22-23 Vers. Vol. 5. N.p.: n.p., n.d. *BibleGateway.com.* Web. 26 Sept. 2016. Amplified Bible (AMP) Copyright © 2015 by The Lockman Foundation, La Habra, CA 90631. All rights reserved.

[7] *Scarface*. Dir. Brian De Palma. Screenplay by Oliver Stone. Perf. Al Pacino. Universal Pictures, 1983. *IFC.com.* 9 Dec. 1983. Web. 26 Sept. 2016. <http://www.ifc.com/2014/05/5-scarface-quotes-that-will-change-your-life>.

[8]"Zig Ziglar." BrainyQuote.com. Xplore Inc, 2016. 26 September 2016. http://www.brainyquote.com/quotes/quotes/z/zigziglar132507.html

[9] "Evander Holyfield." BrainyQuote.com. Xplore Inc, 2016. 28 September 2016. http://www.brainyquote.com/quotes/quotes/e/evanderhol210816.html

[10]*2 Timothy. The Message*. 1-5 Vers. Vol. 3. N.p.: n.p., n.d. *Bible Gateway.* Web. 26 Sept. 2016. <https://www.biblegateway.com/passage/?search=2+timothy+3%3A+2-7&version=MSG>. The Message (MSG) Copyright © 1993, 1994, 1995, 1996, 2000, 2001, 2002 by Eugene H. Peterson

[11] Dr. Seuss." BrainyQuote.com. Xplore Inc, 2016. 29 September 2016. https://www.brainyquote.com/quotes/quotes/d/drseuss105646.html

[12] "Charles Spurgeon." BrainyQuote.com. Xplore Inc, 2016. 29 September 2016. https://www.brainyquote.com/quotes/quotes/c/charlesspu106282.html

**Chapter 3: Integrity**

[1] "integrity". *Dictionary.com Unabridged.* Random House, Inc. 29 Sep. 2016. <Dictionary.com http://www.dictionary.com/browse/integrity>.

[2] *Proverbs. Amplified Bible.* Proverbs 10:9. N.p.: n.p., n.d. *BileGateway.com.* Web. 3 Oct. 2016. <https://www.biblegateway.com/passage/?search=Proverbs+10%3A9&version=AMP>. Amplified Bible (AMP) Copyright © 2015 by The Lockman Foundation, La Habra, CA 90631. All rights reserved.

[3] Bob Marley." BrainyQuote.com. Xplore Inc, 2016. 3 October 2016. https://www.brainyquote.com/quotes/quotes/b/bobmarley578991.html

[4] "John D. MacDonald Quotes." *BrainyQuote*, Xplore, 3 Oct. 2016, www.brainyquote.com/quotes/john_d_macdonald_141376.

[5] *James. New International Version (NIV).* Vol. 4:6. N.p.: n.p., n.d. *BibleGateway.com.* Web. New International Version (NIV) Holy Bible, New International Version®, NIV® Copyright ©1973, 1978, 1984, 2011 by Biblica, Inc.® Used by permission. All rights reserved worldwide.

[6] *James. The Message.* Vol. 11:3. N.p.: n.p., n.d. *BibleGateway.com.* Web. 4 Oct. 2016. he Message (MSG) Copyright © 1993, 1994, 1995, 1996, 2000, 2001, 2002 by Eugene H. Peterson

[7] "W. Clement Stone." BrainyQuote.com. Xplore Inc, 2016. 4 October 2016. https://www.brainyquote.com/quotes/quotes/w/wclements155733.html

[8]*Proverbs. The Message.* Vol. 11:3. N.p.: n.p., n.d. *BibleGateway.com.* Web. 4 Oct. 2016. he Message (MSG) Copyright © 1993, 1994, 1995, 1996, 2000, 2001, 2002 by Eugene H. Peterson

[9]*Job. Amplified Bible.* Vol. 27:4-6. N.p.: n.p., n.d.
*BibleGateway.com.* Web. 4 Oct. 2016. <https://
www.biblegateway.com/passage/?
search=Job+27%3A4-6&version=AMP>. Amplified Bible (AMP)
Copyright © 2015 by The Lockman Foundation, La Habra, CA
90631. All rights reserved.

[10]"Martin Lawrence." BrainyQuote.com. Xplore Inc, 2016. 4
October 2016. https://www.brainyquote.com/quotes/quotes/m/
martinlawr177262.html

[11] "Dwight D. Eisenhower." BrainyQuote.com. Xplore Inc, 2016.
4 October 2016. https://www.brainyquote.com/quotes/quotes/d/
dwightdei109026.html

**Chapter 4: Work Ethic and the Fruits of Labor**

[1] "work ethic". *Dictionary.com Unabridged.* Random House, Inc.
5 Oct. 2016. <Dictionary.com http://www.dictionary.com/browse/
work-ethic>.

[2] fruits of labor. (n.d.) *McGraw-Hill Dictionary of American
Idioms and Phrasal Verbs.* (2002). Retrieved October 5 2016 from
http://idioms.thefreedictionary.com/fruits+of+labor

[3] *2 Thessalonians. The Message.* Vol. 3:10. N.p.: n.p., n.d.
*BibleGateway.com.* Web. 4 Oct. 2016. <https://
www.biblegateway.com/passage/?
search=2+Thessalonians+3%3A10&version=MSG>. The Message
(MSG) Copyright © 1993, 1994, 1995, 1996, 2000, 2001, 2002 by
Eugene H. Peterson

[4] "Will Smith." BrainyQuote.com. Xplore Inc, 2016. 8 October 2016. https://www.brainyquote.com/quotes/quotes/w/ willsmith599824.html

[5] "Thomas A. Edison." BrainyQuote.com. Xplore Inc, 2016. 8 October 2016. https://www.brainyquote.com/quotes/quotes/t/ thomasaed149042.html

[6] "Pope Paul VI." BrainyQuote.com. Xplore Inc, 2016. 8 October 2016. https://www.brainyquote.com/quotes/quotes/p/ popepaulvi120381.html

[7] *Genesis. The Message.* Vol. 2:15. N.p.: n.p., n.d. *BibleGateway.com.* Web. 8 Oct. 2016. The Message (MSG) Copyright © 1993, 1994, 1995, 1996, 2000, 2001, 2002 by Eugene H. Peterson

[8]*Colossians. The Amplified Bible.* Vol. 3:23-24. N.p.: n.p., n.d. *BibleGateway.com.* Web. 8 Oct. 2016. Amplified Bible (AMP) Copyright © 2015 by The Lockman Foundation, La Habra, CA 90631. All rights reserved.

[9] US Census Bureau Public Information Office. "More Young Adults Are Living in Their Parents' Home, Census Bureau Reports -

Families & Households - Newsroom - U.S. Census Bureau." *US Census Bureau Public Information Office*. US Census Bureau, 3 Nov. 2011. Web. 08 Oct. 2016. <http://www.census.gov/newsroom/releases/archives/families_households/cb11-183.html>.

[10] Fry, Richard. "For First Time in Modern Era, Living With Parents Edges Out Other Living Arrangements for 18- to 34-Year-Olds Share Living with Spouse or Partner Continues to Fall." Pew Research Center, May 2016. Web. 9 Oct. 2016. <http://www.pewsocialtrends.org/2016/05/24/for-first-time-in-modern-era-living-with-parents-edges-out-other-living-arrangements-for-18-to-34-year-olds/24>.

[11] Cox, Amanda. "The Rise of Men Who Don't Work, and What They Do Instead." *Www.nytimes.com*. The New York Times, 11 Dec. 2014. Web. 10 Dec. 2016. <http://www.nytimes.com/2014/12/12/upshot/the-rise-of-men-who-dont-work-and-what-they-do-instead.html?_r=0>.

[12] Worland, Justin. "2 in 5 Young Americans Don't Want a Job." *Time*. Time, 14 Nov. 2014. Web. 10 Oct. 2016. <http://time.com/3585786/young-americans-work/>.

[13] Stein, Joel. "Millennials: The Me Me Me Generation." *Time*. Time, 20 May 2013. Web. 10 Oct. 2016. <http://time.com/247/

millennials-the-me-me-me-generation/>.

[14] Fowler, Jeremy. "Sacked! Harrison's Kids Must 'earn a Real Trophy'" *ESPN.com*. ESPN, 17 Aug. 2015. Web. 10 Oct. 2016. <http://www.espn.com/nfl/story/_/id/13447657/james-harrison-pittsburgh-steelers-takes-away-kids-participation-trophies-says-awards-earned>.

[15] *Proverbs. Amplified Bible*. BibleGateway.com, n.d. Web. 10 Oct. 2016. <https://www.biblegateway.com/passage/?search=Proverbs+22:6&version=AMP>. Amplified Bible (AMP) Copyright © 2015 by The Lockman Foundation, La Habra, CA 90631. All rights reserved.

[16] "Mike Rowe." BrainyQuote.com. Xplore Inc, 2016. 10 October 2016. https://www.brainyquote.com/quotes/quotes/m/mikerowe550874.html

[17] "Booker T. Washington." BrainyQuote.com. Xplore Inc, 2016. 10 October 2016. https://www.brainyquote.com/quotes/quotes/b/bookertwa131737.html

[18] "Colin Powell." BrainyQuote.com. Xplore Inc, 2016. 10 October 2016. https://www.brainyquote.com/quotes/quotes/c/

colinpowel121363.html

[19] "Thomas A. Edison." BrainyQuote.com. Xplore Inc, 2016. 10 October 2016. https://www.brainyquote.com/quotes/quotes/t/thomasaed149029.html

[20] *Proverbs. New International Version (NIV)*. BibleGateway.com, n.d. Web. 11 Oct. 2016. <https://www.biblegateway.com/passage/?search=proverbs+12%3A11&version=NIV>. New International Version (NIV) Holy Bible, New International Version®, NIV® Copyright ©1973, 1978, 1984, 2011 by Biblica, Inc.® Used by permission. All rights reserved worldwide.

[21] Kevin Hart." BrainyQuote.com. Xplore Inc, 2016. 11 October 2016. https://www.brainyquote.com/quotes/quotes/k/kevinhart681201.htmly]

[22] *Proverbs. The Message*. BibleGateway.com, n.d. Web. 11 Oct. 2016. <https://www.biblegateway.com/passage/?search=proverbs+24%3A30-35&version=MSG>. The Message (MSG) Copyright © 1993, 1994, 1995, 1996, 2000, 2001, 2002 by Eugene H. Peterson

[23] *Rocky Balboa*. Dir. Sylvester. Stallone. By Sylvester. Stallone.

Perf. Sylvester. Stallone. Metro-Goldwyn-Mayer Pictures Columbia Pictures, 2006. Film.

**Chapter 5: Wisdom**

[1] "wisdom". *Dictionary.com Unabridged*. Random House, Inc. 5 Oct. 2016. <Dictionary.com http://www.dictionary.com/browse/wisdom>.

[2] *Proverbs. Amplified Bible (AMP)*. Vol. 1:7. N.p.: n.p., n.d. *BibleGateway.com*. Web. 12 Oct. 2016. Amplified Bible (AMP) Copyright © 2015 by The Lockman Foundation, La Habra, CA 90631. All rights reserved.

[3] "Albert Einstein." BrainyQuote.com. Xplore Inc, 2016. 12 October 2016. https://www.brainyquote.com/quotes/quotes/a/alberteins148851.html

[4] "knowledge". *Dictionary.com Unabridged*. Random House, Inc. 15 Oct. 2016. <Dictionary.com http://www.dictionary.com/browse/knowledge>.

[5] "information". *Dictionary.com Unabridged*. Random House, Inc. 15 Oct. 2016. <Dictionary.com http://www.dictionary.com/browse/information>.

[6] "logic". *Dictionary.com Unabridged*. Random House, Inc. 15 Oct. 2016. <Dictionary.com http://www.dictionary.com/browse/logic>.

[7] "Confucius." BrainyQuote.com. Xplore Inc, 2016. 14 October 2016. https://www.brainyquote.com/quotes/quotes/c/confucius131984.html

[8] "Calvin Coolidge." BrainyQuote.com. Xplore Inc, 2016. 9

December 2016. https://www.brainyquote.com/quotes/quotes/c/calvincool156506.html

[9]*Proverbs. The Message.* BibleGateway.com, n.d. Web. 17 Oct. 2016. <https://www.biblegateway.com/quicksearch/?qs_version=NIV&quicksearch=Wisdom&begin=66&end=66>. The Message (MSG) Copyright © 1993, 1994, 1995, 1996, 2000, 2001, 2002 by Eugene H. Peterson[i] "common sense". *Dictionary.com Unabridged.* Random House, Inc. 15 Oct. 2016. <Dictionary.com http://www.dictionary.com/browse/common-sense>.

[10] "Common Sense." *Dictionary.com*, Dictionary.com, 17 Oct. 2016, www.dictionary.com/browse/common-sense.

[11]"Nas." BrainyQuote.com. Xplore Inc, 2016. 15 October 2016. https://www.brainyquote.com/quotes/quotes/n/nas569216.html

[12]"Josh Billings." BrainyQuote.com. Xplore Inc, 2016. 17 October 2016. https://www.brainyquote.com/quotes/quotes/j/joshbillin122856.html

[13]By Carlin Flora, Published on May 1, 2007 - Last Reviewed on June 9, 2016. "Gut Almighty." *PsychologyToday.com*. Psychology Today, 9 June 2016. Web. 17 Oct. 2016. <https://www.psychologytoday.com/articles/200705/gut-almighty>.

[14]"Leonardo da Vinci." BrainyQuote.com. Xplore Inc, 2016. 17 October 2016. https://www.brainyquote.com/quotes/quotes/l/leonardoda154281.html

[15] *Proverbs. Amplified Bible (AMP)* "BibleGateway." *Https://Www.biblegateway.com/Passage/?Search=Proverbs+1&Version=AMP*, Bible Gateway Blog, 17 Oct. 2016, www.biblegateway.com/passage/?search=Proverbs%2B1&version=AMP.[

[16] "BibleGateway." James 1 NIV - - Bible Gateway, www.biblegateway.com/passage/? search=James%2B1&version=NIV.

[17] Will Rogers." BrainyQuote.com. Xplore Inc, 2016. 17 October 2016. https://www.brainyquote.com/quotes/quotes/w/ willrogers393513.html

[18] *Matthew. Amplified Bible (AMP(.* BibleGateway.com, n.d. Web. 17 Oct. 2016. <https://www.biblegateway.com/passage/? search=Matthew+26:41&version=AMP>. Amplified Bible (AMP) Copyright © 2015 by The Lockman Foundation, La Habra, CA 90631. All rights reserved.

19] *James. New International Version (NIV).* BibleGateway.com, n.d. Web. 17 Oct. 2016. <https://www.biblegateway.com/ quicksearch/? qs_version=NIV&quicksearch=Wisdom&begin=66&end=66>. New International Version (NIV) Holy Bible, New International Version®, NIV® Copyright ©1973, 1978, 1984, 2011 by Biblica, Inc.® Used by permission. All rights reserved worldwide.

[20] *James. Amplified Bible (AMP).* Vol. 1:7. N.p.: n.p., n.d. *BibleGateway.com.* Web. 12 Oct. 2016. Amplified Bible (AMP) Copyright © 2015 by The Lockman Foundation, La Habra, CA 90631. All rights reserved.

[21] *Forrest Gump.* Dir. Robert Zemeckis. By Eric Roth. Perf. Tom Hanks, Robin Wright, Gary Sinise, Sally Field, and Mykelti Williamson. Paramount Pictures, 1994. Film.

**Chapter 6: Decisiveness**

[1] "decisiveness". *Dictionary.com Unabridged.* Random House, Inc. 5 Oct. 2016. <Dictionary.com http://www.dictionary.com/ browse/decisiveness>.

[2] Maxim Staff. "CLINT EASTWOOD HAS A TOUGH MESSAGE FOR SENSITIVE MILLENIALS." *Maxim.com.* Maxim Magazine, 4 Aug. 2016. Web. 17 Oct. 2016. <http://www.maxim.com/entertainment/clint-eastwood-donald-trump-pussy-generation-2016-8>.

[3] *James. King James Bible.* Vol. 1:8. Nashville, TN: Holman Bible, 1973. Print.

[4]Dixon, Chuck. "Punisher Vol 2 63." *Marvel Database.* N.p., n.d. Web. 18 Oct. 2016. <http://marvel.wikia.com/wiki/Punisher_Vol_2_63>.

[5] *The Karate Kid.* Dir. John G. Advilsen. Screenplay by Robert Mark Kamen. Perf. Ralph Macchio Noriyuki "Pat" Morita Elisabeth Shue. Columbia, Q84. Film.

[6] *Matthew. New International Version (NIV).* BibleGateway.com, n.d. Web. 21 Oct. 2016. <https://www.biblegateway.com/passage/?search=Matthew+5:37&version=NIV>. New International Version (NIV) Holy Bible, New International Version®, NIV® Copyright ©1973, 1978, 1984, 2011 by Biblica, Inc.® Used by permission. All rights reserved worldwide.

[7] *1 Corinthians. King James Bible.* Nashville, TN: Holman Bible, 1973. Print.

[8] *Jeremiah. Amplified Bible (AMP(.* BibleGateway.com, n.d. Web. 21 Oct. 2016. Amplified Bible (AMP) Copyright © 2015 by The Lockman Foundation, La Habra, CA 90631. All rights reserved.

[9] *Psalms. Holy Bible: New Living Translation.* Wheaton, IL: Tyndale House, 1996. Print.

[10] "Napoleon Hill." BrainyQuote.com. Xplore Inc, 2016. 21

October 2016. https://www.brainyquote.com/quotes/quotes/n/
napoleonhi386913.html

[11]William James." BrainyQuote.com. Xplore Inc, 2016. 18
October 2016. https://www.brainyquote.com/quotes/quotes/w/
williamjam386029.html

[12] "Bertrand Russell." BrainyQuote.com. Xplore Inc, 2016. 18
October 2016. https://www.brainyquote.com/quotes/quotes/b/
bertrandru383143.html

[13] *Point Break*. Dir. Kathryn Bigelow. Screenplay by W. Peter Iliff.
Perf. Patrick Swayze, Keanu Reeves, Gary Busey, Lori Petty. 20th
Century Fox, 1991. Film.

[14] "Charles Stanley." BrainyQuote.com. Xplore Inc, 2016. 19
October 2016. https://www.brainyquote.com/quotes/quotes/c/
charlessta451693.html

[15] "Franklin D. Roosevelt." BrainyQuote.com. Xplore Inc, 2016.
19 October 2016. https://www.brainyquote.com/quotes/quotes/f/
franklind109480.html

[16] "Wayne Gretzky." BrainyQuote.com. Xplore Inc, 2016. 19
October 2016. https://www.brainyquote.com/quotes/quotes/w/
waynegretz391237.html

[17] *Proverbs. New Living Translation (NLT)*. BibleGateway.com,
n.d. Web. 19 Oct. 2016. <https://www.biblegateway.com/passage/?
search=proverbs+6%3A4&version=NLT>. New Living Translation
(NLT) Holy Bible, New Living Translation, copyright © 1996, 2004,
2015 by Tyndale House Foundation. Used by permission of Tyndale
House Publishers Inc., Carol Stream, Illinois 60188. All rights
reserved.

[18] "Abraham Lincoln." BrainyQuote.com. Xplore Inc, 2016. 19

October 2016. https://www.brainyquote.com/quotes/quotes/a/
abrahamlin110340.html

[19] "Denzel Washington." BrainyQuote.com. Xplore Inc, 2016. 20
October 2016. https://www.brainyquote.com/quotes/quotes/d/
denzelwash337123.html

[20] *Proverbs. The Message (MSG)*. BibleGateway.com, n.d. Web.
22 Oct. 2016. The Message (MSG) Copyright © 1993, 1994, 1995,
1996, 2000, 2001, 2002 by Eugene H. Peterson

[21] *Galatians. English Standard Version (ESV)*. BibleGateway.com,
n.d. Web. 22 Oct. 2016. English Standard Version (ESV) The Holy
Bible, English Standard Version. ESV® Permanent Text Edition®
(2016). Copyright © 2001 by Crossway Bibles, a publishing
ministry of Good News Publishers.

[22] "Terrence J." BrainyQuote.com. Xplore Inc, 2016. 22 October
2016. https://www.brainyquote.com/quotes/quotes/t/
terrencej498469.html

[23] "Les Brown." BrainyQuote.com. Xplore Inc, 2016. 22 October
2016. https://www.brainyquote.com/quotes/quotes/l/
lesbrown382878.html

[24] *Revelation. New International Version (NIV)*.
BibleGateway.com, n.d. Web. 22 Oct. 2016. <https://
www.biblegateway.com/passage/?
search=Matthew+5:37&version=NIV>. New International Version
(NIV) Holy Bible, New International Version®, NIV® Copyright
©1973, 1978, 1984, 2011 by Biblica, Inc.® Used by permission. All
rights reserved worldwide.

[25] *The Empire Strikes Back*. Dir. Irvin Kershner. By Leigh
Brackett and Lawrence Kasdan. Perf. Mark Hamill, Harrison Ford,
Carrie Fisher, and Billy Dee Williams. Twentieth Century-Fox Film

Corporation, 1980. Film.

[26] Pugachevsky, Julia. "If Ron Swanson Quotes Were Motivational Posters." *BuzzFeed*, BuzzFeed, 6 Oct. 2014, www.buzzfeed.com/juliapugachevsky/if-ron-swanson-quotes-were-motivational-posters.

**Chapter 7: Benevolence**

[1] "benevolence". *Dictionary.com Unabridged.* Random House, Inc. 5 Oct. 2016. <Dictionary.com http://www.dictionary.com/browse/benevolence>.

[2] *1 Corinthians. New Living Translation (NLT).* BibleGateway.com, n.d. Web. 26 Oct. 2016. <https://www.biblegateway.com/passage/?search=1+Corinthians+13&version=NLT>. New Living Translation (NLT) Holy Bible, New Living Translation, copyright © 1996, 2004, 2015 by Tyndale House Foundation. Used by permission of Tyndale House Publishers Inc., Carol Stream, Illinois 60188. All rights reserved.

[3] *James. New Living Translation (NLT).* BibleGateway.com, n.d. Web. 26 Oct. 2016. <https://www.biblegateway.com/passage/?search=1+Corinthians+13&version=NLT>. New Living Translation (NLT) Holy Bible, New Living Translation, copyright © 1996, 2004, 2015 by Tyndale House Foundation. Used by permission of Tyndale House Publishers Inc., Carol Stream, Illinois 60188. All rights reserved.

[4] *James. The Message (MSG).* BibleGateway.com, n.d. Web. 26 Oct. 2016. The Message (MSG) Copyright © 1993, 1994, 1995, 1996, 2000, 2001, 2002 by Eugene H. Peterson

[5] *Matthew. The Message (MSG). Gateway*, Bible Gateway Blog, www.biblegateway.com/passage/?search=Matthew%2B25%3A39-43&version=MSG.

[6] "George Washington Carver." BrainyQuote.com. Xplore Inc, 2016. 26 October 2016. https://www.brainyquote.com/quotes/quotes/g/georgewash106292.html

[7] *John. New International Version (NIV)*. BibleGateway.com, n.d. Web. 26 Oct. 2016. New International Version (NIV) Holy Bible, New International Version®, NIV® Copyright ©1973, 1978, 1984, 2011 by Biblica, Inc.® Used by permission. All rights reserved worldwide.

[8] "Lots of Funny Confucius Quotes, Jokes & Sayings." *Lots of Funny Confucius Quotes, Jokes & Sayings*. Quotescoop.com, n.d. Web. 27 Oct. 2016. <http://www.inspirational-quotes-short-funny-stuff.com/funny-confucius.html>.

[9] "Confucius." BrainyQuote.com. Xplore Inc, 2016. 27 October 2016. https://www.brainyquote.com/quotes/quotes/c/confucius118794.html

[10] *Hebrews. The Message (MSG)*. BibleGateway.com, n.d. Web. 27 Oct. 2016. The Message (MSG) Copyright © 1993, 1994, 1995, 1996, 2000, 2001, 2002 by Eugene H. Peterson

[11] "BibleGateway." James 2:15-17 NLT - - Bible Gateway, www.biblegateway.com/passage/?search=James%2B2%3A15-17&version=NLT.

[12] Tag, By. "A Quote by Mahatma Gandhi." *Goodreads*. N.p., n.d. Web. 27 Oct. 2016. <http://www.goodreads.com/quotes/109910-the-simplest-acts-of-kindness-are-by-far-more-powerful>.

[13] *Romans. Amplified Bible (AMP)*. BibleGateway.com, n.d. Web. 27 Oct. 2016. Amplified Bible (AMP) Copyright © 2015 by The Lockman Foundation, La Habra, CA 90631. All rights reserved. /.latest_citation_text

[14] *Luke. New International Version (NIV).* BibleGateway.com, n.d. Web. 26 Oct. 2016. New International Version (NIV) Holy Bible, New International Version®, NIV® Copyright ©1973, 1978, 1984, 2011 by Biblica, Inc.® Used by permission. All rights reserved worldwide.

[15] *Luke. The Message (MSG).* BibleGateway.com, n.d. Web. 26 Oct. 2016. The Message (MSG) Copyright © 1993, 1994, 1995, 1996, 2000, 2001, 2002 by Eugene H. Peterson

[16] Tag, By. "A Quote by John Bunyan." *Goodreads.* N.p., n.d. Web. 27 Oct. 2016. <http://www.goodreads.com/quotes/41980-you-have-not-lived-today-until-you-have-done-something>.

[17] *John. King James Bible (KJV).* N.p.: n.p., n.d. Print. King James Version (KJV) Public Domain

[18] "William Bennett." BrainyQuote.com. Xplore Inc, 2016. 27 October 2016. https://www.brainyquote.com/quotes/quotes/w/williamben158187.html

[19] *James. Amplified Bible (AMP).* BibleGateway.com, n.d. Web. 27 Oct. 2016. Amplified Bible (AMP) Copyright © 2015 by The Lockman Foundation, La Habra, CA 90631. All rights reserved. /.latest_citation_text

[20]"Horace Mann." BrainyQuote.com. Xplore Inc, 2016. 27 October 2016. https://www.brainyquote.com/quotes/quotes/h/horacemann165981.html

**Chapter 8: Manners and Chivalry**

[1] "manners". *Dictionary.com Unabridged.* Random House, Inc. 5 Oct. 2016. <Dictionary.com http://www.dictionary.com/browse/manners>.

[2] "chivalry". *Dictionary.com Unabridged*. Random House, Inc. 5 Oct. 2016. <Dictionary.com http://www.dictionary.com/browse/ chivalry>.

[3] "Fred Astaire." BrainyQuote.com. Xplore Inc, 2016. 29 October 2016. https://www.brainyquote.com/quotes/quotes/f/ fredastair133199.html
[4]"will.i.am." BrainyQuote.com. Xplore Inc, 2016. 29 October 2016. https://www.brainyquote.com/quotes/quotes/w/ william511045.html

[5] *Luke. The Amplified Bible*. Grand Rapids, MI: Zondervan, 1958. Print. Amplified Bible (AMP) Copyright © 2015 by The Lockman Foundation, La Habra, CA 90631. All rights reserved.

[6] *Titus. The Message (MSG)*. Colorado Springs, CO: NavPress, 2004. Print. he Message (MSG) Copyright © 1993, 1994, 1995, 1996, 2000, 2001, 2002 by Eugene H. Peterson

[7] Roman*s. The Message (MSG)*. Colorado Springs, CO: NavPress, 2004. Print. he Message (MSG) Copyright © 1993, 1994, 1995, 1996, 2000, 2001, 2002 by Eugene H. Peterson

[8] *1 Peter. Holy Bible: Contemporary English Version*. New York: American Bible Society, 1995. Print. Contemporary English Version (CEV) Copyright © 1995 by American Bible Society

[9] *Matthew. Holy Bible: New Living Translation*. Wheaton, IL: Tyndale House, 1996. Print. New Living Translation (NLT) Holy Bible, New Living Translation, copyright © 1996, 2004, 2015 by Tyndale House Foundation. Used by permission of Tyndale House Publishers Inc., Carol Stream, Illinois 60188. All rights reserved.

[10] "William Wilberforce Quotes." *BrainyQuote*, Xplore, 29 Oct. 2016, www.brainyquote.com/quotes/william_wilberforce_618057

[11] "Mike Huckabee." BrainyQuote.com. Xplore Inc, 2016. 29 October 2016. https://www.brainyquote.com/quotes/quotes/m/mikchuckab655165.html

[12] "Justin Timberlake." BrainyQuote.com. Xplore Inc, 2016. 29 October 2016. https://www.brainyquote.com/quotes/quotes/j/justintimb706142.html

[13] H. Jackson Brown, Jr.." BrainyQuote.com. Xplore Inc, 2016. 29 October 2016. https://www.brainyquote.com/quotes/quotes/h/hjacksonb135007.html

[14] "Clarence Thomas." BrainyQuote.com. Xplore Inc, 2016. 29 October 2016. https://www.brainyquote.com/quotes/quotes/c/clarenceth137493.html

[15] LightHouse. "'Manners Maketh Man' - Origin, Meaning, Expansion, Importance." *Important India*, 10 June 2018, www.importantindia.com/23792/manners-maketh-man/.

[16] Washington Free Beacon Staff. "The Best From 'Mad Dog Mattis'." *Washington Free Beacon*. N.p., 18 Mar. 2013. Web. 19 Dec. 2016. <http://freebeacon.com/national-security/the-best-from-mad-dog-mattis/>.

**Chapter 9: Warrior's Mentality**

[1] "warrior". *Dictionary.com Unabridged*. Random House, Inc. 5 Oct. 2016. <Dictionary.com http://www.dictionary.com/browse/warrior>.

[2] "mentality". *Dictionary.com Unabridged*. Random House, Inc. 31 Oct. 2016. <Dictionary.com http://www.dictionary.com/browse/mentality>.

[3] *Braveheart*. Dir. Mel Gibson. Prod. Mel Gibson. By Randall Wallace. Perf. Mel Gibson, Sophie Marceau, and Patrick McGoohan. Paramount Pictures, 1995. Film.

[4] *American Sniper*. Dir. Clint Eastwood. By Jason Hall. Perf. Bradley Cooper, Sienna Miller. Warner Bros. Pictures, 2014. Film.

[5] *Matthew. Amplified Bible (AMP)*. N.p.: n.p., n.d. Print. Amplified Bible (AMP) Copyright © 2015 by The Lockman Foundation, La Habra, CA 90631. All rights reserved.

[6] *Matthew. The Holy Bible: New International Version: NIV*. N.p.: n.p., n.d. Print. New International Version (NIV) Holy Bible, New International Version®, NIV® Copyright ©1973, 1978, 1984, 2011 by Biblica, Inc.® Used by permission. All rights reserved worldwide.

[7] *Luke. Holy Bible: English Standard Version (ESV)*. London: Collins, 2009. Print. English Standard Version (ESV) The Holy Bible, English Standard Version. ESV® Permanent Text Edition® (2016). Copyright © 2001 by Crossway Bibles, a publishing ministry of Good News Publishers.

[8] *Enter The Dragon*. Dir. Robert Clouse. By Michael Allin. Perf. Bruce Lee, John Saxon, Ahna Capr,i Robert Wall, Shih Kien, Jim Kelly, Bolo Yeung. Warner Bros. Pictures, Golden Harvest, 1973. DVD.

[9] "Chuck Norris." BrainyQuote.com. Xplore Inc, 2016. 31 October 2016. https://www.brainyquote.com/quotes/quotes/c/chucknorri379783.html

[10] *Psalms. The Message (MSG)*. Colorado Springs, CO: NavPress, 2004. Print. The Message (MSG) Copyright © 1993, 1994, 1995, 1996, 2000, 2001, 2002 by Eugene H. Peterson

[11] George S. Patton." BrainyQuote.com. Xplore Inc, 2016. 2 November 2016. https://www.brainyquote.com/quotes/quotes/g/georgespa104742.html

[12] "Carlos Castaneda Quote." *A-Z Quotes*. Azquotes.com, n.d. Web. 02 Nov. 2016. <http://www.azquotes.com/quote/571674>.

[13] "Harry S Truman." BrainyQuote.com. Xplore Inc, 2016. 2 November 2016. https://www.brainyquote.com/quotes/quotes/h/harrystrum121205.html

[14] *2 Timothy. Amplified Bible (AMP)*. N.p.: n.p., n.d. Print. Amplified Bible (AMP) Copyright © 2015 by The Lockman Foundation, La Habra, CA 90631. All rights reserved.

[15] *1 Corinthians Amplified Bible (AMP)*. N.p.: n.p., n.d. Print. Amplified Bible (AMP) Copyright © 2015 by The Lockman Foundation, La Habra, CA 90631. All rights reserved.

[16] "John C. Maxwell." BrainyQuote.com. Xplore Inc, 2016. 3 November 2016. https://www.brainyquote.com/quotes/quotes/j/johncmaxw600921.html

[17]"Edmund Burke." BrainyQuote.com. Xplore Inc, 2016. 31 October 2016. https://www.brainyquote.com/quotes/quotes/e/edmundburk377528.html"Geo

[18]"Ronald Reagan." BrainyQuote.com. Xplore Inc, 2017. 2 January 2017. https://www.brainyquote.com/quotes/quotes/r/ronaldreag169550.html

[19] *1Peter. The Holy Bible: New International Version: NIV*. N.p.: n.p., n.d. Print. New International Version (NIV) Holy Bible, New International Version®, NIV® Copyright ©1973, 1978, 1984, 2011 by Biblica, Inc.® Used by permission. All rights reserved worldwide.

[20] George S. Patton." BrainyQuote.com. Xplore Inc, 2016. 2 November 2016. https://www.brainyquote.com/quotes/quotes/g/georgespa104742.html

[21] *Captain America: Civil War*. Dir. Anthony & Joe Russo. Screenplay by Christopher Markus and Stephen McFeely. Perf. Chris Evans, Robert Downey Jr., Scarlett Johansson, Sebastian Stan, Anthony Mackie, Don Cheadle, Jeremy Renner, Chadwick Boseman, Paul Bettany, Elizabeth Olsen, Paul Rudd. 2016. Film.

[22] Niemöller, Martin, Pastor. "Martin Niemöller: "First They Came for the Socialists..."" *United States Holocaust Memorial Museum*. United States Holocaust Memorial Council, 02 July 2016. Web. 06 Nov. 2016. <https://www.ushmm.org/wlc/en/article.php?ModuleId=10007392>.

[23]"Ronald Reagan." BrainyQuote.com. Xplore Inc, 2017. 2 January 2017. https://www.brainyquote.com/quotes/quotes/r/ronaldreag169550.html

[24] *Braveheart*. Dir. Mel Gibson. Prod. Mel Gibson. By Randall Wallace. Perf. Mel Gibson, Sophie Marceau, and Patrick McGoohan. Paramount Pictures, 1995. Film.

## Chapter 10: Humility

[1] "humility". *Dictionary.com Unabridged*. Random House, Inc. 8 Nov. 2016. <Dictionary.com http://www.dictionary.com/browse/humility>.

[2] "George Clooney." BrainyQuote.com. Xplore Inc, 2016. 9 November 2016. https://www.brainyquote.com/quotes/quotes/g/georgecloo578167.html

[3] *Proverbs. Amplified Bible (AMP)*. N.p.: n.p., n.d. Print. Amplified Bible (AMP) Copyright © 2015 by The Lockman

Foundation, La Habra, CA 90631. All rights reserved.

[4] "Michael J. Fox." BrainyQuote.com. Xplore Inc, 2016. 9 November 2016. https://www.brainyquote.com/quotes/quotes/m/ michaeljf585842.html

[5]"Steven Tyler." BrainyQuote.com. Xplore Inc, 2016. 9 November 2016. https://www.brainyquote.com/quotes/quotes/s/ steventyle361972.html

[6] *1 Peter. Amplified Bible (AMP)*. N.p.: n.p., n.d. Print. Amplified Bible (AMP) Copyright © 2015 by The Lockman Foundation, La Habra, CA 90631. All rights reserved.

[7] "Tim Tebow." *BrainyQuote*, Xplore, 9 Dec. 2016, www.brainyquote.com/search_results?q=tim%2Btebow.

[8] "BibleGateway." *Proverbs 27:6 AMP - - Bible Gateway*, www.biblegateway.com/passage/? search=Proverbs%2B27%3A6&version=AMP.

[9] "LeBron James." BrainyQuote.com. Xplore Inc, 2016. 9 November 2016. https://www.brainyquote.com/quotes/quotes/l/ lebronjame425360.html

[10] *The Holy Bible: New International Version: NIV*. Cambridge: Cambridge UP, 2013. Print. ew International Version (NIV) Holy Bible, New International Version®, NIV® Copyright ©1973, 1978, 1984, 2011 by Biblica, Inc.® Used by permission. All rights reserved worldwide.

[11] "Rick Warren." BrainyQuote.com. Xplore Inc, 2016. 9 November 2016. https://www.brainyquote.com/quotes/quotes/r/ rickwarren395865.html

[12] "Dwayne Johnson." BrainyQuote.com. Xplore Inc, 2016. 9

November 2016. https://www.brainyquote.com/quotes/quotes/d/
dwaynejohn760904.html

[13] "John Madden." BrainyQuote.com. Xplore Inc, 2016. 9
November 2016. https://www.brainyquote.com/quotes/quotes/j/
johnmadden158609.html

[14] "John Wooden." BrainyQuote.com. Xplore Inc, 2016. 9
November 2016. https://www.brainyquote.com/quotes/quotes/j/
johnwooden386606.html

**Chapter 11: Forgiveness**

[1]"forgive". *Dictionary.com Unabridged*. Random House, Inc. 8
Nov. 2016. <Dictionary.com http://www.dictionary.com/browse/
forgive>.

[2] "Mahatma Gandhi." BrainyQuote.com. Xplore Inc, 2016. 14
November 2016. https://www.brainyquote.com/quotes/quotes/m/
mahatmagan121411.html

[3]"Bruce Lee." BrainyQuote.com. Xplore Inc, 2016. 14 November
2016. https://www.brainyquote.com/quotes/quotes/b/
brucelee383809.html

[4] "Alexander Pope." BrainyQuote.com. Xplore Inc, 2016. 14
November 2016. https://www.brainyquote.com/quotes/quotes/a/
alexanderp101451.html

[5] *1 John. The Holy Bible: New International Version: NIV*.
Cambridge: Cambridge UP, 2013. Print. New International Version
(NIV) Holy Bible, New International Version®, NIV® Copyright
©1973, 1978, 1984, 2011 by Biblica, Inc.® Used by permission. All
rights reserved worldwide.

[6] *Psalm. The Holy Bible: New International Version: NIV*.

Cambridge: Cambridge UP, 2013. Print. New International Version (NIV) Holy Bible, New International Version®, NIV® Copyright ©1973, 1978, 1984, 2011 by Biblica, Inc.® Used by permission. All rights reserved worldwide.

[7] *Galatians. The Holy Bible: New International Version: NIV.* Cambridge: Cambridge UP, 2013. Print. New International Version (NIV) Holy Bible, New International Version®, NIV® Copyright ©1973, 1978, 1984, 2011 by Biblica, Inc.® Used by permission. All rights reserved worldwide.

[8]"Brennan Manning." BrainyQuote.com. Xplore Inc, 2016. 14 November 2016. https://www.brainyquote.com/quotes/quotes/b/brennanman531771.html

[9] "Tyler Perry." BrainyQuote.com. Xplore Inc, 2016. 14 November 2016. https://www.brainyquote.com/quotes/quotes/t/tylerperry561197.html

[10] *Matthew, Holy Bible: New Living Translation.* Wheaton, IL: Tyndale House, 1996. Print. New Living Translation (NLT) Holy Bible, New Living Translation, copyright © 1996, 2004, 2015 by Tyndale House Foundation. Used by permission of Tyndale House Publishers Inc., Carol Stream, Illinois 60188. All rights reserved.

11] *Matthew. The Message (MSG).* N.p.: n.p., n.d. Print. The Message (MSG) Copyright © 1993, 1994, 1995, 1996, 2000, 2001, 2002 by Eugene H. Peterson

[12] "Rick Warren." BrainyQuote.com. Xplore Inc, 2016. 14 November 2016. https://www.brainyquote.com/quotes/quotes/r/rickwarren394615.html

[13] *Luke. The Message (MSG).* N.p.: n.p., n.d. Print. The Message (MSG) Copyright © 1993, 1994, 1995, 1996, 2000, 2001, 2002 by Eugene H. Peterson

[14] *Romans, Holy Bible: New Living Translation.* Wheaton, IL: Tyndale House, 1996. Print. New Living Translation (NLT) Holy Bible, New Living Translation, copyright © 1996, 2004, 2015 by Tyndale House Foundation. Used by permission of Tyndale House Publishers Inc., Carol Stream, Illinois 60188. All rights reserved.

[15]"Oscar Wilde." BrainyQuote.com. Xplore Inc, 2016. 14 November 2016. https://www.brainyquote.com/quotes/quotes/o/oscarwilde105222.html

[16] "Lewis B. Smedes." BrainyQuote.com. Xplore Inc, 2016. 14 November 2016. https://www.brainyquote.com/quotes/quotes/l/lewisbsme135524.html

[17] "Mark Wahlberg." BrainyQuote.com. Xplore Inc, 2016. 14 November 2016. https://www.brainyquote.com/quotes/quotes/m/markwahlbe471079.html

[18] "Lex Luger." BrainyQuote.com. Xplore Inc, 2016. 14 November 2016. https://www.brainyquote.com/quotes/quotes/l/lexluger566428.html

[19] "Bernard Meltzer." BrainyQuote.com. Xplore Inc, 2016. 14 November 2016. https://www.brainyquote.com/quotes/quotes/b/bernardmel132866.html

[20] Keith, Kent M., Dr. "The Paradoxical Commandments - by Kent M. Keith." *The Paradoxical Commandments - by Kent M. Keith.* KentMKeith.com, 1968. Web. 14 Nov. 2016. <http://www.kentmkeith.com/commandments.html>.

## Chapter 12: Accountability And Loyalty

[1] "accountability". *Dictionary.com Unabridged.* Random House, Inc. 26 Oct. 2016. <Dictionary.com http://www.dictionary.com/

browse/accountability>.

[2] "accountable". *Dictionary.com Unabridged*. Random House, Inc. 26 Oct. 2016. <Dictionary.com http://www.dictionary.com/browse/ accountable>.

[3] "loyalty". *Dictionary.com Unabridged*. Random House, Inc. 19 Nov. 2016. <Dictionary.com http://www.dictionary.com/browse/ loyalty>.

[4] @PsychToday, and Todd B. Kashdan, PPh.D. "Why Do Men Have a Hard Time Making Friends?" *Psychology Today*. N.p., 24 Oct. 2011. Web. 19 Nov. 2016. <https://www.psychologytoday.com/ blog/curious/201110/why-do-men-have-hard-time-making-friends>.

[5] Tom Price." BrainyQuote.com. Xplore Inc, 2016. 19 November 2016. https://www.brainyquote.com/quotes/quotes/t/ tomprice622514.html

[6]*Proverbs. Amplified Bible (AMP)*. N.p.: n.p., n.d. Print. Amplified Bible (AMP) Copyright © 2015 by The Lockman Foundation, La Habra, CA 90631. All rights reserved.

[7] *James. The Message (MSG)*. Colorado Springs, CO: NavPress, 2004. Print. The Message (MSG) Copyright © 1993, 1994, 1995, 1996, 2000, 2001, 2002 by Eugene H. Peterson

[8] "Stephen Covey." BrainyQuote.com. Xplore Inc, 2016. 19 November 2016. https://www.brainyquote.com/quotes/quotes/s/ stephencov636497.html

[9] "Ernie Banks." BrainyQuote.com. Xplore Inc, 2016. 19 November 2016. https://www.brainyquote.com/quotes/quotes/e/ erniebanks371053.html

[10] *Proverbs*. New Living Translation (NLT) Holy Bible, New

Living Translation, copyright © 1996, 2004, 2015 by Tyndale House Foundation. Used by permission of Tyndale House Publishers Inc., Carol Stream, Illinois 60188. All rights reserved

[11] "Tommy Lasorda." BrainyQuote.com. Xplore Inc, 2016. 19 November 2016. https://www.brainyquote.com/quotes/quotes/t/tommylasor610866.html

[12]Szoldra, Paul. "19 Unforgettable Quotes from Legendary Marine Gen. James 'Mad Dog' Mattis." *Business Insider*. Business Insider, Inc, 20 Nov. 2016. Web. 21 Nov. 2016. <http://www.businessinsider.com/general-mattiss-best-quotes-2016-11/#you-cannot-allow-any-of-your-people-to-avoid-the-brutal-facts-if-they-start-living-in-a-dream-world-its-going-to-be-bad-1>.

[13]"John Cena." BrainyQuote.com. Xplore Inc, 2016. 19 November 2016. https://www.brainyquote.com/quotes/quotes/j/johncena513459.html

[14] "Stephen Baldwin." BrainyQuote.com. Xplore Inc, 2016. 19 November 2016. https://www.brainyquote.com/quotes/quotes/s/stephenbal582939.html

[15] *Romans. The Holy Bible: New International Version: NIV*. Cambridge: Cambridge UP, 2013. Print. New International Version (NIV) Holy Bible, New International Version®, NIV® Copyright ©1973, 1978, 1984, 2011 by Biblica, Inc.® Used by permission. All rights reserved worldwide.

[16] "Herschel Walker." BrainyQuote.com. Xplore Inc, 2016. 19 November 2016. https://www.brainyquote.com/quotes/quotes/h/herschelwa266263.htm

[17]*The Hangover*. Dir. Todd Phillips. By Jon Lucas and Scott Moore. Perf. Radley Cooper, Ed Helms, Zach Galifianakis, Heather Graham, Justin Bartha, Jeffrey Tambor. Warner Bros., 2009.

## Parting Shots

{1] *Philippians. Message Bible: The Message of Christmas.* Place of Publication Not Identified: Tyndale House, 2014. Print. Copyright © 1993, 1994, 1995, 1996, 2000, 2001, 2002 by Eugene H. Peterson

[2] *James. Amplified Bible (AMP).* N.p.: n.p., n.d. Print. Copyright © 2015 by The Lockman Foundation, La Habra, CA 90631. All rights reserved.

[3] *Man Of Steel.* Dir. Zack Snyder. By David S. Goyer. Perf. Henry Cavill, Amy Adams, Michael Shannon, Kevin Costner, Diane Lane, Laurence Fishburne, Russell Crowe. Warner Bros.Pictures, 2013. Film.

[4] *Spider-Man.* Dir. SamRaimi. Screenplay by Scott Rosenberg, Alvin Sargent, and James Cameron. Perf. Tobey Maguire, Willem Dafoe, Kirsten Dunst, James Franco. Columbia TriStar Home Entertainment, 2002. Film.

[5] *1 Corinthians. Holy Bible: English Standard Version.* Wheaton, IL: Crossway Bibles, 2001. Print. The Holy Bible, English Standard Version. ESV® Permanent Text Edition® (2016). Copyright © 2001 by Crossway Bibles, a publishing ministry of Good News Publishers.

[6] Thompson, Hunter S. "A Quote from The Proud Highway." *Goodreads.* GoodReads.com, n.d. Web. 17 Jan. 2017. <http://www.goodreads.com/quotes/47188-life-should-not-be-a-journey-to-the-grave-with>.

[7] "BibleGateway." 1 Corinthians *13:11 NIV - - Bible Gateway,* www.biblegateway.com/passage/?search=Acts%2B20%3A24&version=NIV.

Made in the USA
Monee, IL
26 May 2021